PREACHING THROUGH
THE CHRISTIAN YEAR

3

PREACHING THROUGH THE CHRISTIAN YEAR

3

Sermon outlines for the Seasons of the Church's Year

George Reindorp

MOWBRAYS
LONDON & OXFORD

ISBN 0 264 64611 8

First Published 1973
by A. R. Mowbray & Co Ltd
The Alden Press, Osney Mead,
Oxford, OX2 oEG

Text set in 12/13 pt. Monotype Bembo, printed by letterpress,
and bound in Great Britain at The Pitman Press, Bath

PREFACE

We are ordained to preach. The Ordinal makes that clear. 'Take thou authority to preach the Word of God . . . '

So I am one of the thousands of Priests, Readers and Ministers of our own and other communions at home and abroad who owe a debt of gratitude to Douglas Cleverley Ford. When, therefore, Messrs Mowbray told me that it was with his encouragement that they invited me to contribute to this series of sermon outlines I was glad to accept. His advice at the outset, his constructive criticisms during compilation and his writing of the Introduction place me further in his debt.

Sermons in these days may be at Parish Communion, Morning and Evening Prayer or some other service; and the length of time available varies considerably. I have had this much in mind as the length of some of the outlines shows.

Research among parish priests seems to indicate that special services are on the increase, when a body of people (schools, nurses and doctors, old people, marriage reunion, etc., etc.,) come to their parish church. At such times parish priests are naturally anxious to rise to the occasion, and many tell me that a sermon outline to meet this need would be especially helpful. I have included eleven of these.

One of the advantages of serving on a large staff first as a curate, later as an incumbent, and then being Provost of a Cathedral, is that of hearing a large number of other people preach. (An inestimable benefit denied, alas, to a bishop whose appearance without a sermon, or at least a 'few words' would be regarded as almost a breach of contract!) As it happens, I find it easy to memorise illustrations and quotations of prose and poetry when I hear other people use them in the pulpit. But the source of these may not be mentioned and subsequent research prove unavailing. May I, therefore, apologise to any whose ideas I have plagiarised or copyright infringed.

The last sermon, 'Growing old gracefully', has a special history for me. It is based on one I heard my father deliver when he was 85 years old. Strangely enough he seems to have broken his invariable custom—throughout sixty years of ministry—of typing every word of his sermons, together with an index of text, subject and place of delivery. I have all these, but can find no trace of this one. If, therefore, I have wrongly clothed the skeleton of his main points I doubt if those in Paradise bother much about copyright.

I can, however, here gladly acknowledge my gratitude to Messrs Hodder & Stoughton, who allowed me to use in part or whole some of the material I have written in my books *What about You, Over to You, No Common Task;* and who also publish my *Ten Points for Preachers* to which Douglas Cleverley Ford refers in his Introduction.

My secretary, Muriel Barnes, retains my friends for me by sparing them my handwriting and typing these outlines.

I offer this book in the hope that, despite the relentless demands that preaching makes on us clergy in the modern world, it may be of help to those who believe as I do that we are bound to give of our best in telling out the good news of the Gospel of Christ.

✠ *George Sarum*

CONTENTS

Part Three. Sermons for Special Occasions

INTRODUCTION

I am glad that the Bishop of Salisbury responded to the publisher's invitation, and my invitation, to write the third volume in our series *Preaching Through the Christian Year*. Not because he is a bishop, though I am happy to have a bishop helping us in this field. Not because I have known him for many years; we were actually in the same bunch of ordinands in St Paul's Cathedral on Trinity Sunday 1937. Not even because he has a reputation as a preacher. I put forward his name because I know him to have the heart of a priest.

If ever a parish should find itself in the unfortunate position of having to choose between a preacher or a priest for its vicar, I would advise it to choose the priest. And for this reason, that the priest is concerned about people, he understands people, how they think, the way they feel and what they can manage. A priest is like a father. He is willing to stoop down, to take people by the hand, to encourage first steps, even if they are small and uncertain steps, to provide practical support, to make use of organisations and material objects, to involve those he is trying to help in individual and corporate action. A father knows, a priest knows, that children cannot run before they can walk, but the aim is to get them to run, and this they will only achieve if they are encouraged to try on their own.

The author of this book of sermon outlines preaches with the heart of a priest. Who else in the sermon called 'Another Way' would have thought of a confirmation candidate, or a communicant, coming forward to meet Christ up 'the centre aisle' and returning to his seat by the side aisle—another way! But this is how ordinary people catch hold of spiritual truth, which is abstract. And there is the story about the little girl reaching for the tempting jar of jelly on the high shelf in the larder.

A preacher who is a good priest knows how to 'earth' sermons. In theological terms he has grasped the principles of the Incarnation, the Word has become flesh and dwelt among us. He has also grasped the sacramental principle, how the material can become the vehicle of the spiritual. These basic theological understandings lead the competent preacher on to further techniques which enable the content of his message to be received. Each sermon has one theme or aim and the evidence of this is the fact that each sermon can readily be given a title. Moreover, each *section* of the sermon can be given a heading. These headings would not normally appear in a sermon script but I asked the author to insert them in this book in order to demonstrate the connection between the various sections of the sermon. If sub-headings cannot readily be supplied to sections of a sermon, each bearing some relation to the overall title, there is something drastically wrong with the sermon.

Personality affects preaching. Of course it does if in preaching the Word is to become flesh. But it is personality in which the Christ is operative. The preacher is the Lord's witness in his person. Readers of this book will encounter George Reindorp in his sermons. If I did not think this were so I should have rejected the original manuscript. But the sermons are Christocentric. There is no doubt about the Person whom the preacher proclaims. There is not only Kerygma, however, though very properly it is the connecting thread of the whole book, but there is also Didache, Catachesis and Paraclesis. This is because the preacher has the heart of a priest. Moreover, the hearers of this preaching are expected to do something as a result of what they hear.

Teachers of preaching in Germany divide the subject into two main heads—Homiletik and Rhetorik. The homiletical aspect of the sermons in this book is obvious. What is not clear and could not be clear without hearing him 'live' is the preacher's mastery of Rhetorik (which means speaking style). For this I commend his little book, *Ten Points for Preachers*. The Bishop of Salisbury does not fall down on delivery. Content cannot neglect Form. Homiletik cannot dispense with Rhetorik.

I am happy to be able to include this book in our series for I am confident that it will make a distinctive contribution to the ministry of the Word which so much needs strengthening in the total ministry of the Church today.

D. W. Cleverley Ford

Part One. Church Seasons

ADVENT

Conscience

'Should I do this? Ought I do that? It's against my conscience.'

You've heard people say sentences like this hundreds of times. You've said them yourself. Are you quite sure you know what you mean when you talk about conscience?

As everyone has a conscience, we certainly ought to know something about it. And we all experience great difficulty at times in deciding which of several sources of action is the right one.

1. *Conscience as a voice*

I want you to look at three very different scenes.

(a) The first is a court scene—the prisoner at the bar is speaking and everyone is hanging on his words. The governor, sitting as judge, surrounded as he is by his captains and his guards, seems ill at ease. Conflicting emotions are at war within him. The prisoner's speech goes on. And then, in the account of the trial we read: 'And as Paul reasoned of righteousness, temperance and judgement to come, Felix trembled.' 'Trembled' or—in the Greek original—'was terrified'.

A judge 'terrified' by the voice of the prisoner at the bar? Why? Is it possible perhaps that the prisoner's voice speaks in unison with another voice audible to none but Felix himself— a voice coming from his own heart?

(b) The second scene is from one of the world's greatest short stories.

A young man is penniless, his money squandered in a bout of wild extravagance, his friends gone, his future hopeless. Glad to do anything he gets a job keeping pigs. And then, when 'he came to himself', when he was utterly alone, when for the first time since he left home he could listen to another voice that seemed to call him he made a resolution: 'I will arise and go to my father.'

(c) Years after that story was told the third scene took place in Lorraine.

A young country girl is proposing to set out from her tiny village to the Court to set the weakling prince firmly on his throne and to raise the siege of Orleans. And she proposes to do all this—which seems madness to her own folk—in obedience to voices she claims to have heard.

Now where do these voices come from which were heard so clearly by the Roman Governor, Felix, the Prodigal Son and the Peasant Maid? If you had asked Joan of Arc she would have said simply: 'I hear voices telling me what to do. They come from God.'

If you had asked the psalmist he would reply: 'The Lord even the most mighty God hath spoken.'

> A light, a guide, a warning,
> A presence ever near,
> Through the deep silence of the flesh
> I reach the inward ear.
>
> (J. G. Whittier)

Conscience—the voice of God in the soul of man. It was the voice of God in his soul that caused Felix, the hardened world-ling to tremble.

It is his, 'that gentle voice we hear' that makes us, like the prodigal son, turn again to our Father. It is God's voice that calls men and women to follow him.

2. Conscience as universal

Now the first thing to notice about conscience is its universality. Everyone has a conscience. We glibly say of somebody (though never to ourselves!) 'How could he do that, he's got no conscience!' But it is an empty figure of speech. For even if we ignore the voice of God in nature, in the Bible, and in his Son, man cannot get away from his own conscience.

Some time ago I saw a play in which a man and his conscience appeared on the stage together. There were two men, dressed exactly alike, walking about and talking aloud to each other just as we talk to our own conscience. When the man wanted to do something which he knew perfectly well wasn't right, he read aloud to his conscience long boring columns from the newspaper in the hope that he would send his conscience to sleep and then be able heedlessly to follow his own lusts.

But conscience can't be got rid of in this fashion. It can't be explained away. The voice of God in the soul of man speaks with too commanding a voice for this.

The philosopher Kant said two things filled him with awe, the starry heavens at night and the moral law within. And every Christian as he hears the voice of conscience, warning, advising, leading, checking, knows that through that voice the most mighty God hath spoken.

But if it is true that everyone has a conscience it is equally true that everyone's conscience needs educating.

We must be sure that the still small voice of God is not swallowed up in the earthquake of overmastering ambitions or the fire of selfish passion. The whole of the Old Testament is without meaning unless we see it in the gradual education of conscience. So, too, later on. We cannot doubt, for example, that the people who carried out the Inquisition were quite conscientious people; they really thought it was right to burn a man's body to save his soul. Down to our own day God has been educating us as nations and individuals on questions of slavery and slums.

3. Conscience in need of correction

How, then can conscience be educated? We can take three maxims from the lives of the saints.

(a) First, be still, and then listen. Do you know those people who rush into your room and say: 'I want to ask your advice, I've decided to do so-and-so'? Well, of course, they don't want

5

your advice, they don't want to hear what you've got to say—they just want an audience for their own schemes.

I think we're rather like that with God. First we have to be still and listen for God's voice. And what better time than the time Christ chose, early in the morning?

(b) Second, talk to the great teacher of your soul till your will and his unite in wonderful communion. There's no better way of educating your conscience than by the daily prayers that are part of a Christian's everyday life.

(c) Third, follow as closely as you can in the steps of the Good Shepherd, so that soon by instinct you will come to know the voice that is his and his alone.

ADVENT

The royal law

The Bible

Do you remember the Coronation? Or perhaps you have seen pictures of it?

Immediately after the Queen was crowned by the Archbishop of Canterbury the Moderator of the Church of Scotland received a copy of the Holy Bible from the High Altar and, presenting it to Her Majesty, said these words:

'Receive this Book, the most valuable thing this world affords. This is the Royal Law. These are the Lively Oracles of God.'

Some people have a real knowledge of their Bible from regular reading and study. Others are sentimentally attached to it recognising certain passages when they hear them, while the copy they had at school collects dust on a shelf. Others feel that much of what it says has been debunked or disproved and doubt its value.

Where do you stand?

We Christians call our Bible the 'Word of God'. For us it is no magical book which fell out of heaven. It is no dedicated script written down for our especial benefit. It is not a text book which answers all questions about Man, God and the Universe. But it is that book, that place which man can consult for guidance, inspiration, authority and instruction. Above all it is the only source book we have for the deeds and words of Jesus, giving us, we believe, an authentic picture of what God is like.

What Christ said

There is a story of a collection of people who were getting near heaven when they came to a cross roads. One arm of the signpost said: 'To Heaven'. The other said: 'To a lecture on Heaven'. And they all went off to the lecture! So many people will tell you what this newspaper or that declares that Christ said; what St Paul is supposed to have thought about women wearing hats in church; how many animals went into the ark; but far too few have ever read in the Bible what Christ actually did say.

You should be one of those few. If therefore you mean business, here's a suggestion for you this Advent.

Take a Bible. Turn to one of the Gospels in the New Testament—St Mark. Borrow a red pencil. Underline in red Christ's own words. Then when you've done that, read them through. Don't worry about the verses or chapter headings or anything else. Altogether they will only be the length of a few columns in your favourite newspaper. Try and get the spirit behind his words and the general purpose of his life. Note what he says about God and what he is like. I believe that when you have done this; when you have read what he said, how he lived, died and rose, three things will stand out in your mind:
(a) God is a Father;
(b) Christ is always talking about a new age, a new kingdom;
(c) He wants *you*, the best in you, to help in achieving this new age.

What Christ says to you

It is this feeling of God wanting me that keeps Christianity alive. It is because millions of ordinary men and women have this experience—call it religious experience if you will—that they dare to call themselves Christians. The hangers-on of religion, the more or less half-and-half Christians, the charming 'pagans' who retain some strain of half-forgotten Christianity so as to be thought 'respectable'—all these are really people who get warmth from a fire. They are not on fire themselves. They are as much to do with real religion as the bride's veil has to do with being in love. The true sources of any real religious vitality are people who have themselves experienced this call from God, however reluctant they would be to put it into words.

So take your Bible, God's book for everyman. Study this call from God which millions have heard. This Advent God may speak to you . . .

ADVENT

The Call

'Do you think in your heart, that you be truly called according to the will of our Lord Jesus Christ and the order of this Church of England, to the order and Ministry of the Priesthood?' asks the bishop, of the ordinand.

Why do you think it is that too few men seem to be hearing or responding to this call?

I believe that the whole attitude towards vocation is desperately lacking in many quarters. I do not mean simply of vocation to the sacred ministry, but towards vocation. The highest, most Christian, job for everyone is the job he is clearly meant to do. God certainly does not reserve the best Christians for the sacred ministry. He wants the best Christians in every job. He wants the doctor who remembers that his patients have souls as well as bodies; he wants the Christian MP who tries to promote good laws in Parliament; he wants the Christian mother who does wonderful church work in bringing up a thoroughly happy and devoted family to God's glory; he wants Christian grandparents who have learnt the difficult art of growing old gracefully—

these are the people who are alive to their vocation—they are doing the job that God wants them to do with all their might.

The parson's job

What then, briefly, are the main functions of the parson's job? To be prophet, priest, pastor.

1. *A prophet*

First the parson must be a prophet. He must know that it is the voice of God which thunders from Mount Sinai; it is the spirit of God which inspires prophets great and small to proclaim the eternal message of justice, truth and freedom. He must know that it is the voice of the God who will come again to judge; the word of the God who sustains a myriad worlds by the breath of his power. 'Thus saith the Lord' must always be the refrain of the parson. It is his privilege to tell out, sometimes with 'stammering lips and another tongue', the great truths which God has revealed to men. Not for him to state his own opinions. Good news from God is the commission with which the parson is entrusted. Humiliating as it must always be to preach to the children of God, it is the inescapable duty of the parson—and he must not fail. He must be a prophet.

2. *A priest*

He must be a priest. Pavlova was asked by someone what one of her dances meant and replied: 'If I could have said it, do you suppose I should have troubled to dance it?' Worship in fact is the highest activity of which man is capable. Worship is response. In the heart of every man there is a throne and there is an altar; and whatever god we place upon the throne will determine the quality of the offering we make upon the altar. Man can in no lesser way express what God is worth. In this activity of his whole self, in this activity of the whole family, the priest must lead. Note that he strives to do all in his power not to stand between his people and God, but so to lead them with him that together they approach the throne of grace. If the priest is a man of prayer so will the family be. If the priest is a man who makes frequent communion with God so will the family be.

'I wish you every happiness in your new job' wrote Dr Derbyshire, the then Archbishop of Cape Town to a priest returning to England after the war. 'If some circumstances make the use of vestments inadvisable do not worry too much. Too many of us have thought that people would be taught by "eyegate" in this matter. Far more important and urgent is to let them see what richness there is in the sacrament of the altar. Most people are influenced if they see how much it means to their parson and in their parson's life.'

3. A pastor

Yes, the parson must be a prophet and also a priest.

Then, too, he must be a pastor. This function has never been better described than in the Queen's Regulations and Admiralty Instructions for the duties of a Chaplain . . . 'The friend and adviser of all on board.' It is a high ideal and makes stern demands. He must never be too busy to give his best to individuals. A ring at the bell so often seems an interruption, when really of course it is a case of 'the Master hath come and calleth for thee'. People matter. He is the under-shepherd, and to the Chief Shepherd the flock matter; because he has bought them, and they are his, infinitely precious, and to be *loved into* the bosom of the family when only loving will bring them home to God.

Prayer for a parson

So pray with me for those known to you whom God has called to this terrifying and glorious ministry. Pray that more men may be found, please God, to lead his people. They must be priests, standing before God, to be used for his worship and his work. They must be pastors, feeding the flock and caring for those redeemed by his precious Blood. They must be evangelists, forsaking the temptation to cuddle their faith to their bosom, surrounded by a holy coterie of cassock-clinging admirers, and going out into the clatter and bustle of the world to seek and save that which is lost. They must be fearless, ready and able to lead as Christ led his flock. Not afraid to be definite, to take a stand, to issue a challenge. They must be men under authority. Ready to obey orders, as they promised at their ordination. And if their obedience to their vows grows dim, if self-conceit or puffed-up vanity make them disobedient, then pray more earnestly that they may be drawn again to him who made them for himself.

Perhaps you wonder what the priest prays when he mounts the pulpit steps. I will tell you what one says:

> When I stand up to preach to those,
> Whose goodness and humility
> Rebuke me, till I flinch with fear,
> Christ of the Mountain, look on me.
>
> (Charles W. Hutchinson)

ADVENT

Death

A vicar had just preached a sermon on 'Life after Death'. In the vestry afterwards he said: 'Well, Mr Churchwarden, what do you think will happen to you when you die?'

'I suppose I shall go to everlasting bliss, vicar, but I wish you wouldn't talk about such unpleasant subjects!'

Here was a churchwarden who wouldn't face facts. Many people take after him. Christians however must be realists. Christ was a realist. Of course we don't want to be morbidly curious about death, and certainly not gloomy; but we all have to face it sooner or later, for ourselves and for those we love.

To many people it presents one of the great difficulties of the Christian faith. That is why we must think about it.

There seem to be three main questions everyone is always asking when they have to meet death face to face, or watch their loved ones die. First, is death the end? Second, shall we see again those we love? Third, what is our relation with those who have gone?

Is death the end?

Many would answer 'yes'. When you're dead you're dead. But it is 'in the sight of the unwise that the souls of the righteous seem to die.' In the sight and sure faith of the Christian they are in the hand of God and at peace. Read Chapter 15 of his first letter to the Corinthians, and see whether you cannot make St Paul's great statement your own: 'If the dead are not raised neither hath Christ been raised; and if Christ hath not been raised your faith is vain.' For the Christian hope is not one of mere human survival.

The only argument for human immortality which our Lord is known to have used is his answer to the unbelieving Sadducees: 'God is not the God of the dead but of the living, for all live unto Him.' Belief in God is primary, belief in human immortality is secondary. The second stands or falls by the first, 'Because I live you shall live also.'

Shall we see again those we love?

A god who planted in me deep affections, bound me with cords of love to those whom I hold dearest in this world, and then in one sudden moment in a capricious whim smashed those bonds and let them crumble in my hands—he could never be my saviour; he could never be the father of Jesus Christ.

An old lady of 94 died after a life of loving devotion to a large family. If you asked one of her sons if he would see his mother again, he would reply, 'If God did not let me see my mother again, God would have cheated me, and God doesn't behave like that'. That is the answer of unswerving faith, of loving trust in God who is faithful, who understands our human loves because he is himself their source and inspiration.

And because you accept him as Lord of this world and of that which is to come—Lord of life, death and life eternal—you do not seek to peer through the dark door of the body's death. Do not fear that among the 'multitude which no man can number' your loved ones will be swallowed up. For when the question rings out, 'What are these and whence come they?', back comes the answer, 'Sir, thou knowest . . . for the Lord knoweth them that are his.' Enough for you that Jesus said, 'Today shalt thou be with me in Paradise.' He is saying, 'I am looking after your loved ones for you. They are safe and happy with me. Nothing can my power withstand, none can pluck them from my hand.'

What is our relation with those who have gone?

This question is another way of asking: 'What do we mean by the communion of saints?' We mean a communion of those still in the body with those who have passed through the body and gone. The choice of the word 'communion' is a happy one. The highest communion of all is one without words, because it rises above words. The spiritualist demands communication. The Christian is content with communion, which is higher, closer, more intimate than communication. Communion is fellowship, spirit with spirit.

> I watch thee from the quiet shore,
> Thy spirit up to mine can reach
> But in dear words of human speech
> We two communicate no more.

'God forbid' says Augustine, writing about his mother, 'that in a higher state of existence she should cease to think of me, to long to comfort me, she who loved me more than words can tell.'

Is it not then right and natural that we should continue to pray for those whom we love but see no longer? Prayer is an act of faith in God's love. We release his power into other lives. We rejoice in the communion of saints:

> O blest communion, fellowship divine!
> We feebly struggle, they in glory shine;
> Yet all are one in Thee, for all are Thine.
> (Bishop W. Walsham How)

And because 'all are thine', death cannot kill the love that binds us all together in a bond that transcends time and space, and lifts us above them both into the life of God himself.

13

CHRISTMAS

Home and family

His Christmas was in a Nazi prison cell. He knew that the only way out was through death by slow torture or being murdered in cold blood.

He wrote a wedding sermon. In it Dietrich Bonhoeffer said:
'Most people have forgotten nowadays what a home can mean, though some of us have come to realise it as never before.

'It is a kingdom of its own in the midst of the world, a haven of refuge amid the turmoil of our age, nay more, a sanctuary. It is not founded on the shifting sands of private and public life, but has its peace in God. For it is God who gives it its special meaning and dignity and worth. It is an ordinance God has established in the world, the place where peace, quietness, joy, love, purity, continence, respect, obedience, tradition and, to crown all, happiness may dwell, whatever else may pass away in the world.'

Few would deny his definition. All would wish to enjoy that sort of home.

Are our homes like that? Are English homes like that? Is yours? What do *you* think?

Setting standards

The strings of family life were inevitably loosened by two world wars but in war the State took upon itself the role of disciplinarian and the nation, in fact, became one large family.

But after the war a Welfare State was created overnight. Individuals and families could receive an endless series of benefits, some deserved, some undeserved, some necessary, some unnecessary, but nearly all available without the needful exhibition of any personal or family responsibility and discipline.

Faced with such a take-over bid by the State, it is not surprising that the lamps started to go out in the family windows. Parents shrugged their shoulders, turned blind eyes, closed the shutters, and left it all to someone else.

Against this background what do we expect—what do we

deserve to expect from today's adolescents and young people? And please note that the background has been created by us and not by them.

It is we adults who have failed to give standards. Yes, of course, our children would kick against them. But they would have something to kick against. It is when you have nothing to kick against that you fall flat on your face.

For myself I have little but undying admiration for the majority of young people—the vast majority—who having tasted the fruits of the environment we have created for them, have come through unscathed, and are useful members of society with a high sense of responsibility even if it has been painfully acquired by trial and error. They have a compassion for the homeless, the starving, the under-privileged at home and abroad that shames our own complacency; and a determination to live their own lives in their own way.

How few of them are able to walk in the light of a lamp lit in a home which is secure and stable because it is rich in shared affection, mutual responsibility, strong in religious beliefs and national pride—a home that is a 'lamp unto their feet and light unto their paths.'

Is your home like that? Do you want it to be? I do. I want it to be 'out of this world' and Christmas makes it so.

The festival of the family

For Christmas for me *is* out of this world. You see it began out of this world. It is a love story. God so loved that he gave—he sent his son to come into our world, to have a name and address in Bethlehem, like mine in Salisbury. So love came down at Christmas. And Christmas for me and my family begins at midnight on Christmas Eve, the night before he was born.

There are stars in the sky and magic in the air. Like you I've had different homes. Perhaps I'm in a cruiser in mid-Atlantic. Perhaps I am in hospital. Perhaps I'm in a church or cathedral. There's stillness, low lights, low voices, no music yet—the world is waiting—the great thanksgiving, the Midnight Eucharist is about to begin.

Everyone is there, vast chunks of the human family. Stock-brokers, accountants, schoolboys and jockeys, nuns and news-paper men, monks and models, nurses with their red cloaks warming the white of their uniform, old tired faces who have seen much in the past, children's bright eyes looking into the future, mothers and fathers, children and grandparents, my fellow Christians the world over, all joined close to you and me by a golden chain of prayer . . . all come to join the shepherds, to see the star, to hear the angels, to join the crowd, yet be quite alone around the manger.

> Hark the herald angels sing,
> Christ is born in Bethlehem.

My home

Then back home and when the rest of the day begins, there are stockings and presents and laughter, paper caps and crackers and silly jokes, and the dog and still more magic.

What is this magic? Is it because everyone seems a little kinder, a little gayer, a little lovelier than they are for 364 days?

Is it because the children round us proclaim that parenthood is infinitely worthwhile?

It is this and much more. It is great gulps of gratitude for home and hearth, for food and friendship, prayers for those whom the world shuts out—as they shut him out too.

It is because of what our eyes see and our heart tells us that the needs of individual souls the world over can be offered to our God through Jesus Christ. The caring of a Welfare State, the caring of great organisations for refugees and displaced persons, the caring of human beings like you and me for those we love, the caring of parents for children with real sacrifice, restraint and understanding in the home—all these are a pale reflection of the caring of the God who taught the world what caring really meant, what it costs to come and live and love and die for loving.

So as the angels' song fades and the day dies, I start out again down the road of life, with a star to guide me and a song in my heart, and when they ask me whether my God cares about the world in which he made his home, despite all I see around, I simply say:

'Love came down at Christmas. My God is like that.'

CHRISTMAS

Stooping down

It was Mary first. Mary of Magdala. Mary with the red hair. Mary who'd been a woman of the streets. Christ found her. Christ won her. Now he was dead and buried. In a new tomb. She stood outside weeping. And as she wept she stooped down and looked in. He wasn't there. He had risen. She told Peter. He ran. He stooped and went in. It was true. He'd risen. 'Where is he now?' asks Pilate's wife in fear. 'Gone lady', answers the centurion, 'gone into the world where no man can touch him.' But that was later.

Before Mary it was John. John the Baptist. John clothed with camel's hair, wild, unruly, prophetic. He cries: 'There cometh one mightier than I after me, the latchet of whose shoes I am not worthy to stoop down and unloose.' But that, too, was later.

God stoops

But what before both John and Mary?—GOD!—God beyond the furthest star, God the creator and sustainer of the universe, God outside time and space, God the eternal, who deigned to come and break into time, into our world, and *stooping down* became a child in a cattle stall for you and me.

The result? Peace on earth did you say? They're stooping down today in many places because if they don't stoop someone will blow their head off.

They're stooping down in the Middle East, Jew and Arab, lest each might see or shoot the other.

They're stooping down in India and Pakistan to count, per-chance to recognise, one of the half million dead who may be their brother, mother, sister, father, child.

They're stooping down in Ulster behind a shield, or a tank, or wall because so-called Christians hate each other. Peace!

> Thy Peace! Thou pale, despisèd Christ
> What Peace is there in Thee,
> Nailed to the Cross that crowns the world
> In agony?
> What Peace was Thine? Misunderstood,
> Rejected by Thine own,
> Pacing Thy grim Gethsemane,
> Out-cast and lone.
>
> (G. A. Studdert-Kennedy)

News

And yet, can't you hear . . .

> . . . angels bending near the earth
> To touch their harps of gold:
> Still through the cloven skies they come,
> With peaceful wings unfurled;
> And still the heavenly music floats
> O'er all the weary world:
> Above its sad and lowly plains
> They stoop on hovering wing;
> And ever o'er its Babel-sounds
> The blessed angels sing.
>
> (E. H. Sears)

They bring news of a God who serves. A message which thrusts the Christian into a life of serving in whatever way the world needs serving. It speaks of healing to the sick, forgiveness to the guilty, leaping with joy to the lame, sight to the blind, freedom to those in captivity in mind or body. It speaks to prisoners of inner freedom. But it also means working for prison reform and better parole systems and rehabilitation where you and I live. It speaks of working as a hospital aide, nurse, doctor, as a proclamation of news to the sick. It speaks of working in the political order and exercising your vote and your influence, forming public opinion to secure adequate incomes for the poor and protecting the dignity of men. It speaks of caring about and taking action about the Third World. It means proclaiming with conviction where you work and where you live the power of Jesus.

Getting down to it

Will you do it? Where you work? Where you live? In your school? In your neighbourhood? To do it you'll have to stoop. Your religion must be down to earth. As a Christian you must keep your eyes focused on the world and the needs of those outside the Church. The news you have to spread is good news sent by God, sometimes acted out by Christians, sometimes discovered in the world outside the Church. Evangelism for you and me is a 'go' word, not a 'come' word. We put the integrity of our message in danger when we measure its authenticity by the size of the response. Worse still, we expose ourselves to great temptation to manipulate people when we measure our faithfulness by how our hearers respond.

> It was Mary first.
> Then Peter.
> Before that John Baptist.
> Now it's you and you and you and me.

But you'll have to sink a lot of pride. You'll have to start again. You'll have to hate less and love more. You'll have to stoop to see the child in the manger. To learn his mind, to see his face, to serve him well.

> He came down to earth from heaven.
> For us,
> Will you kneel and adore . . . stooping down . . . NOW?

19

NEW YEAR

The woman who looked back

'Remember Lots wife' (Luke 17.32)

New Year's Day. Tomorrow, today will be yesterday. And yesterday was last year. So the present is but a moving line between the past and the future. So remember Lot's wife. 'Her name is not known but a piece of her shroud is in every home'. So runs the clue of the crossword puzzle when the solution is 'Lot's wife'. She has the shortest biography in history, the curt account of the calamity that befell the second woman in the Bible who was disobedient. 'But Lot's wife, behind him, looked back and she turned into a pillar of salt'.

Youth

In our youth we thought we could do as we liked with life. We soon discovered that our powers were very limited. Nevertheless life gave us growing strength and wider scope for activity. Then middle age sets in—what the psalmist calls 'the sickness that destroyeth in the noonday'. Hardening of the arteries of the conscience tempt us to declare that it will be best in the few remaining years of our life to resist change, to acquiesce in what life offers and let it take its course. Then Christ reminds us about Lot's wife. Christians have to write in their hearts that every day is Doomsday, a day of judgement, a day when by coming one day nearer death we rejoice in eternal life. For the use of history is to give value to the present hour and its duty.

> The best is yet to be
> That last of life for which the first was made
> Our times are in his hand
> Who saith: 'A whole I planned
> Youth sees but half: trust God: see all: nor be afraid.
>
> (Robert Browning)

Growing old gracefully

To those who are trying in the evening of their lives to practise this difficult art, Lot's wife has a clear message. 'Don't bury your heart with the dead and live in the past. You believe in the communion of saints and you and your loved ones are together at the altar. Don't spend your time sighing for the days that won't come again. Bring all the resources of your long experience to the problems of today'.

'Don't bother about us, Vicar', said the remarkable Mrs Potter, then some 90 years young, when I first became her parish priest. 'We've been lucky, brought up in the faith and survived two wars at least. Concentrate on the young and we will pray you through.'

So like her, give your increasing leisure to the prayers that need not now be crowded out; prayers for so many you may know who will never pray for themselves, but who in the good providence of God may come to the Celestial City carried by no prayers but yours.

Hard questions

But as you start this New Year determine to ask yourself some straight questions. What will you say to your fellow travellers on the Christian road about men, women and ministry? What will you say about stewardship? Will your song be of the rise in the cost of living or the rise in your wage and your salary? What will you personally think, pray and do about our fellow Christians in West Africa rising to new efforts of reconciliation and reconstruction which flow from Christ the great healer? When they were 'spotlighted' in war you cared much. And now? Immigration, industrial relations . . . where do you as a Christian stand?

The future

So as Christians on New Year's Day, look ahead. Don't wallow in past sins and omissions that litter your life and Church history. If you do, the grace of your religion, your parish life the life of your synod may become a thing that is dead, fossilized, frozen, an inanimate monument to what might have been. All around you are a generation of next-comers who will listen to you if you are young at heart and can harness their great compassion and sincerity to a religion that attracts with Christ's' likeness. Their eyes watch you more than you think. So, whoever you are, whatever your age, whatever your gifts, the Christian must be . . .

> One who never turned his back but
> marched breast forward,
> Never doubted clouds would break,
> Never dreamed, though right were worsted,
> wrong would triumph,
> Held we fall to rise, are baffled to
> fight better,
> Sleep to wake.

So wrote Robert Browning. But it was Christ who said: 'Remember Lot's wife'.

EPIPHANY

Another way

'And being warned of God in a dream that they should not return to Herod, they departed into their own country another way.' (Matt. 2.12.)

Another way. Let's go home another way. Why? Well, it's more interesting. Is that it? Not in Ireland, or Vietnam or parts of the Middle East. You go home another way lest an enemy or a sniper follows your tracks and is bent on murder.

Not from Bethlehem. You go home another way lest Herod may meet you and be bent on murder of the young child you've been to see. Then you're glad to go home another way. After what they'd seen the Magi felt that nothing would ever be the same again. They wouldn't be the same. The world wouldn't be the same. They had seen Christ.

Not the same

You'll come up to be confirmed. You will kneel. In response to the prayers of the Church and your friends God the Holy Spirit will come through the simple act of the laying on of hands to dwell in your heart. You will go back to your place. You go back another way. You go back another person. You look the same. You may feel the same. But there will be a difference. Will anyone notice it? Will God?

You come up to the altar by the centre aisle. You make your communion. You go back to your seat down the side aisle. You go back 'another way'. After what you've done, nothing will ever be quite the same again. You won't be the same. You have seen Christ, fed on him in your heart by faith with thanksgiving.

Did people notice anything about the Magi, the three Wise Men, the three Kings—call them what you will—when they got back to their own country? Back to the same old street, same old work, same old temptations. I'm sure they did. Men thought they'd 'got something'—though they might not be able to explain what.

It wasn't just the excitement of hearing all about their journey. It took two years, across 600 miles of desert, across the river Euphrates, the visit to the palace, the disappointment; the next stage, the stable, the faces of the mother and the baby. No, they themselves were different. Men 'took knowledge of them that they had been with Jesus.' What they received was— CHRIST.

Resulting action

'This meeting is a waste of time', said someone who was trying to restart a Youth Club which had been closed. 'You've got the same people back again; you can't change human nature.' How right he was, and how hopelessly wrong. He couldn't change

23

human nature. Nor can I. Nor can you. But God can. Ask the old Papuan Christian who as a boy watched his father and uncles at their cannibal sacrifices. Ask the wise men as they returned—returned by another way—returned to another vision of what life was about. Ask the man or woman or the confirmation candidate who's made their first confession. They return by another way, for another start. They can't go on just coming to church and perhaps grumbling about what's wrong with the world, or the Church, or their friends and relations. They've got to do something about it where they work and where they live. Men notice they've 'got something'—Christ.

So have you.

CONVERSION OF ST PAUL

A single-minded man

'*One thing I do*' (Philippians 3.13)

INTRODUCTION

Most of us like to think we are very busy people. Do you notice how our salesmen friends usually begin the overture of their remarks with the phrase, 'Of course, I know you're a very busy man, sir', as if that were a subtle form of flattery. And let us admit it, who would be prepared to confess that their department of a store, or business house, has less to do than the next one? Or watch the faces of departmental heads of the Civil Service when it is suggested that their department should be cut down in any way. Or, if you really want to make an acid test, suggest to Mrs X that she has far less to do than her next door neighbour Mrs Y. If looks could kill your death would be sealed!

Yes, we all like to think we are very busy people, with a long list of duties.

But I defy you to think of a busier man than the dynamic personality who wrote the words of our text: '*One* thing I do'.

A busy man

Let us think about some—only a few of Paul's activities. Remember he had a trained mind, schooled at home in Tarsus, then sent to the university to study under the great teacher Gamaliel. There he acquired that indefinable something which characterises the varsity man. Not—as some critics would idly believe—a string of letters after his name, but the ability to think independently, to value learning for its own sake, not its commercial value, and above all to make friends with people with whose views on almost everything he entirely disagrees— an invaluable asset for a prophet, a priest and, I suggest, for a cabinet minister or a man-in-the-street. Yet here was no mere theorist. Like all orthodox Jews he was taught a trade, a tent-maker. Living in a Greek-speaking city in Asia Minor, a university town, a port, a caravan city, a big lumber and spinning centre, he was used to mixing with merchants and sailors and people from everywhere; used to speaking the world-wide language—Greek. Thoroughly at home in a boat, his seamanship could not be derided.

Picture him then, with his immense energy, persuasive power of speech, first-class mind, tough body, an outstanding man in any company of people, virile, striking, a leader of men.

Of his fiery persecution of these ridiculous Christians every-one knew. It was common talk. So was his dramatic conversion on the Damascus Road. Everyone was talking about it, old university friends, servants, traders, seamen—and the story lost nothing in the telling we may be sure.

His activities

Then began one of the greatest campaigns, the most whirlwind crusade in history.

Perhaps when you were at school you were made to follow, as most of us were, the seemingly tedious missionary journeys of St Paul, cramming into your head isolated incidents connected with each place.

How different was the reality!

Watch Paul as he rouses the enthusiasm of converts all over

the world. Watch him organising a little band here, encouraging a laggard there. Feel with him in his affectionate greetings: 'God is my witness how I long after you all' . . . in his impetuous temper with these fool Galatians, of his love for his fellow countrymen . . . 'I would be willing to be accursed from Christ for the sake of the brethren.'

Mark, too, the little personal touches. He sent his love to Rufus and his mother—'who was also a mother to me' and you see the gratitude of a lonely man to a dear kindly old lady who has mothered him. Hear the clank of the chains as, bound to a Roman soldier, he writes 'Remember my bonds'. Or read the exquisite and courteous note to Philemon whose young slave had robbed him, run off to Rome to have a good time and there met Paul. Paul won him to religion, and had grown to love him dearly. Back to his employer he sent him with the note: 'Receive him, he is my child, Onesimus whom I have begotten in my bonds. I will repay the money.'

And apart from all this, yet one with it, are his letters dictated to a secretary, full of passionate zeal for Christianity, yet so balanced in their wisdom that they have come down to us enshrined in our Bible, full of that wisdom which is old yet ever new.

His fate

Could such a man hope to go unopposed?

Thrice stoned, thrice shipwrecked, five times scourged, adrift in an open boat, in peril of robbers and assassins, exhausted by labour, constantly imprisoned—all these were but the daily accompaniments of the life of this amazing man.

And now the end is near. He is under arrest at Rome. Martyrdom seems inevitable after such a life; at times it seems desirable. To him comes Epaphroditus from Philippi. They could never forget him—nor he them—for of all his converts they were the most dear. So with the deepest conviction he sends them a last note. Wouldn't you have thought that he might be fully justified in recounting at least some of the many ways in which he had discharged his task? Surely now, he will review the life which has been so full of teeming activity, surely he will speak of his past cares and duties—manifold as they are? Does he?

'One thing I do.'

His example

Singleness of mind, singleness of purpose. You see it in the mind of Adolf Hitler, as he strives for world domination at whatever cost. There it is stark and devilish. You see it in Joan of Arc as she follows unswervingly the call of her voices. There it is impelling. You see it as the Captain of the 'Jervis Bay' turns his ship towards the enemy, courting death for the protection of his convoy. There it is glorious.

It takes many forms. The woman at her cradle, the man of science at his instruments, the ploughman at his furrow, the young and old when they love and worship . . . the ordinary man and woman when, despite the derision of the modern world, they press on, a way marked by the steps of the Son of God.

Singleness of mind, some call it. Jesus called it purity of heart.

And those who cherish it . . .

'Happy are the pure in heart, for they shall see God.'

QUINQUAGESIMA

Two mottoes

'God so loved the world'

Poised on one foot in the middle of Westminster's fair city there twinkles a mischievous boy. His body is bent, following the course of his sped arrow from his clasped bow.

Country cousins up to see the sights call him a 'Little Love', a 'Darling'. Exuberant students regard him as the hub of their hubbub, and at times of coronation or great national events he wears a gilded cage to protect him from the antics of over-grown school-boys.

Prostitutes and perverts frequent his domain on lustful pleasure bent.

Stop the roar of London's traffic and ask anyone the boy's name. 'Why, it's Eros, of course, the God of Love, you know.' Few know his brothers, Pothos, Himeros—longing and desire. Fewer still know the motto on the crest of the whole family—two words: I want.

Another motto

Not poised on one foot, but hanging from three nails outside Jerusalem's fair city there hung a young man. His body was wracked. In his hand no bow, in his side the wounds of a spear. Country cousins up to see the sights had called him a prophet, a good man. Students had found a match for their wit and knowledge. No gilded cage protected him, but a crown of thorns adorned him.

Prostitutes frequented his path on lustful pleasure bent. They left him to become saints, the precious ointment of their heart poured forth in searing penitence.

Stop the roar of Jerusalem's traffic and ask any of the swirling crowd the young man's name. 'Why it's Jesus, Jesus of Nazareth whom some thought to be the Son of God.' Few knew his friends, scattered and dismayed. Fewer still now know the motto on the breast of this God of Love—two words:

I give.

The contrast

Eros—God of Love—as pagans called him. Motto, I want. Christ—God of Love—as Christians call him. Motto, I give. The love story, the love interest, free love, self-love, passion, lust, these are the courtiers which people the kingdom of Eros. Self-sacrifice, selflessness, self-denial, self-disicipline, are the courtiers which people the kingdom of Christ.

Here then defined is the charity about which Christ showed us, Paul wrote of and one of the great collects of the Anglican liturgy speaks.

Some would wrongly have us believe that Christian charity is something mawkish and sentimental. Others that it is a pleasant tolerance towards other people. Others again link it with the presentation of Christianity that forgets the hard bits, thrives on popularity and rejoices in organisations and clubs that only demand a vaguely religious background and an occasional nod to God.

But we have 'not so learned Christ'. The dying crimson of his blood was not poured out in a pool of sentimentality. It was freely shed for greater things. For from the heart of God there flows a charity that loves not merely the lovable and attractive, but reaches out to the degraded and dull, the unbearable and vile—in fact to you and me. Such is the charity of God.

Three trees

Three trees once grew on a hillside; and as they swayed in the breeze they would dream what they would like to be.

'I should like to be cut down one day', said the first tree, 'and turned into a baby's cradle.'

'I should like to be cut down one day', said the second tree, 'and become a great ship sailing the seas, carrying treasure and precious stones.'

Said the third: 'I should just like to stand on a hill top and point people to God.'

One day the woodcutters came along and cut down the first tree. 'Let's make it into a cattle stall', they said. 'But I don't want to be a cattle stall', cried the tree, 'I want to be a baby's cradle.' But they turned it into a cattle stall. And when the child Jesus was born they laid him gently in the cattle stall for there was nowhere else to lay him. And the tree said: 'Why, this is far, far more wonderful than ever I dreamed.'

The woodcutters felled the second tree. 'Let's make this tree into a fishing boat', they said. But the tree said, 'I don't want to be a fishing boat. I want to be a great ship carrying treasure and precious stones.' But they turned the tree into a fishing boat and put it on an inland lake. A fisherman called Simon Peter bought the boat and Jesus sailed in the boat and taught the people from it. And the tree said: 'Why, this is far, far more wonderful than ever I dreamed.'

Of the third tree they said, 'Let's make it into a cross'. But the tree said: 'I don't want to be a cross, a thing of shame where men die. I want to stand on a hill top and point people to God.' But they turned the tree into a cross and Jesus was nailed to the cross: and all down the ages men have looked to that cross which has pointed them to God.

So God loved the world.

LENT

What has Christianity to say?

Christianity is a way of walking not talking, a way of living; and its most convincing answers to rivals must always be given in the sphere of practice. But conduct rests on creed, politics or theology. What I believe governs what I do. So the first question about Christian conduct is not 'What must I do?' but 'What is God like?'

Here are four great shattering truths that Christianity has to say to the world.

(a) First, the fundamental Christian assertion is that God reigns and loves. God is not a name for an impersonal power. He is a living God. He is the Lord and not the prisoner of the laws which he has made for the government of the universe. Though many inhabitants of one or more of his innumerable worlds are in rebellion against him, he still reigns. The nations before him are 'as a drop in a bucket'.

(b) Secondly, to the question: 'How can we know what God is like?' Christianity boldly answers: 'Through Jesus Christ our Lord'. There for all time, for all to see, in the express image of God's person, came Christ.

He came into the very stuff of our world. He took flesh, he

had a name and address, lived, loved, died, rose and is alive for evermore. To every question which begins: 'Why did God . . . ?' Christianity answers: Why did Christ?' 'What does God think about this?' Christianity says: 'What did Christ think about this?' There in Christ we see the nature of God. In the written records you have the historical evidence of what Christ did, said, and believed. There for all time you have the picture of what God is like.

(c) Thirdly, Christianity proclaims that man has sinned. Christians are realists—like Christ. They call a spade a spade. They admit failure. Mr Twentieth-Century does not. Christians admit failure. They call it sin. Mr Twentieth-Century describes a frenzied mob of young hooligans bent on destruction and acting like ill-disciplined soldiers as an interesting example of free activity and self-expression. Christianity calls it sin. Mr Twentieth-Century sees a man desert his wife and children and go off with another woman as his mistress and calls it a 'point of view'. Christianity calls it sin. But do not get the idea that Christians are first concerned with the censorious denunciation of the sins of others. Not they! They are far too conscious of their own secret sins, less public and spectacular perhaps, but no less real. But Christianity proclaims that God, the timeless One, chose to take upon himself your sins and mine.

Christianity says you will not get what you deserve. Christianity says you will not reap the wages of sin which is death. Christianity says you will have life, real life, life here and hereafter; because he lives, we shall live also—alive to God through Christ our Lord.

(d) Lastly, Christianity proclaims that here and now there is a visible fellowship which men and women the world over are invited to join to serve God in his work for the redemption of mankind. Make no mistake. This is not a holy-huddle of cassock-clingers, men and women of pious mien counting candles and cuddling their own souls. This is an army in which you and I are called upon to fight against the other army of co-operative guilt and limited liability which the New Testament calls the 'world'.

These are the four great truths which Christianity has to proclaim. These truths are either the truth, not about religion but about life itself, or they are the grossest lies that have ever been foisted on a troubled world. Which are they?

LENT

What faith means

Some time ago a train stopped at a certain station and into the carriage got a young man whose open-necked shirt and walking-stick foretold a day in the country. The four occupants already settled in their corners eyed the newcomer with that passive hostility which people seem to reserve for anyone who dares to disturb the peace of their own particular compartment. Hardly had the train started again and the four occupants returned to the study of their newspapers than the brakes were applied, the train came to a standstill and there followed one of those long inexplicable silences only understood by those versed in the running of a railway. At last someone broke the silence of English reserve and conversation soon became general. It dealt with railways as a whole, went on to other topics, settling finally on newspapers and the Press.

'Look at this article', said one man pointing to his own paper ... "Have we lost our faith?" What on earth does that mean?'

'That's rather interesting,' replied his neighbour, 'we were saying at home the other night that every time we go to church the parson tells us that we must have faith, but he never tells us what it is or how to get it. I'd like to ask everyone sitting in the church I go to what the word "faith" means to them.'

'So would I', replied the first speaker.

'Why not write a note and ask your parson to preach about it?' broke in the newcomer, speaking for the first time. There was no answer. 'At any rate,' he went on, 'I'll take the hint myself and preach about it next Sunday.'

'Are you a parson?' said four voices in unison.

'Yes.'

'Oh'—was the reply, said in just that tone which the average Englishman reserves for talking to small children, lunatics and parsons he doesn't know.

So let's deal with their question straight away.

If you ask me to define 'faith' I would give you two definitions. One—by a famous theologian: 'Faith is an experiment that ends in experience.' The other simpler: 'Faith is trust in a person, and that person is God.'

Now we must be quite clear on one point. This faith, this trust in God is a matter of the whole man acting single-heartedly under the leadership of a dominant purpose. The intellect, the emotions and the will all have their part to play, but although we can consider those parts separately they cannot really be isolated.

(a) *Intellect*

What part does the intellect play? If I walk into a child's nursery and find letters of the alphabet scattered on the floor, the formation of even the shortest word is enough to show me that some mind has been at work. If that conclusion is a trick of mind, then all deduction is at an end, including the deductions of science.

In the universe I find words. Some events seem as meaningless as letters dropped on a nursery floor; but even I, a child of the universe, can read some of the words. The word 'goodness', for instance, I can stumblingly understand. I can't read all the words, of course, but even one would be enough to show that in this universe a mind has been at work. Is it less than mine? It cannot be. The highest things I have—personality and some discernment of a sense of values—must be possessed by that greater mind. So I think I am driven to speak of a personal God. And since even I can see that love is greater than hate and kindness than cruelty, I begin to postulate a good God.

(b) *Will*

So far the intellect has been my guide, the leader of my faith.

But perhaps it does not seem to get me far enough. My own thinking is not sufficient. What contribution shall my will make? I call in the specialists who in this matter are the saints. I find that their opinion has a unanimity not found by specialists in any other branch of human enquiry. They have said that God is good and that man's highest function is to adore him.

Now suppose I went to a great medical specialist for a consultation. When he pronounced his opinion I shouldn't begin to say, 'But haven't you forgotten this, or what about that?' I should accept his opinion. So, too, I accept the unanimous opinion of the saints. How much more do I accept the opinion of the greatest religious genius of all time, Jesus Christ? Can anyone argue with a genius on his own subject? And Christ's subject was God. And on the cross he called him 'Father'. So when a bereaved mother cries out, 'Why did God take my baby?', it is my will that forbids me to accept that cry; it is my will that drives me to go on striving even in the face of the darkest tragedies. For I trust in a Person, in a God who is a Father, who is good, even though his ways pass man's understanding, for his thoughts are higher than my thoughts.

(c) *Emotion*

What of the emotions? What part does feeling play in faith? 'Mysticism', as we call it, and the inner life of the spirit are common to all of us in a greater or less degree, and our feelings seem to us the deepest and most vivid of all our experiences. While we obviously have to guard against unchecked and worthless emotions, the genuineness of what we may call 'religious experience' can never be doubted. All of us have at some time or other heard that still small voice. All of us have felt the presence of God.

CONCLUSION

So then faith is an act of the whole man—emotion, intellect, will—not just one side of our nature.

It begins as a longing to find some meaning in life behind the stress of change and chance. It is—as the writer in the epistle to the Hebrews says—'the assurance of things hoped for, the proving of things not seen'. Christianity, it has been well said, is a way of walking not of talking, and so faith comes into its own by being lived. We have to accept the limitations which debar us from complete knowledge, for a curtain seems to hang between us and the eternal world. But here in this world we often say about some situation or crisis which has arisen: 'If only X were here I shouldn't worry, everything would be all right.' So, too, the Christian tries not to be tossed about by every wind of opinion that comes along, but goes forward in faith with courage and steadfastness echoing the words of Shaw's Joan of Arc: 'His friendship will not fail me, nor His counsel, nor His love. In His strength I will dare and dare and dare till I die. And so God be with me.'

LENT

Why the church?

Parsons often receive anonymous letters. Usually they find their way pretty quickly into the waste-paper basket. But I've always kept one. This is what it said:

'Dear Padre,
    I must admit frankly that I have not been to church for eleven years, but I have been hearing you these last three Sundays. You've been all right so far, but next Sunday I see you're talking about "Why the Church?" Let me tell you you're on a very sticky wicket!
                    Yours,
                        Inquiring Mind.'

Now I believe there are lots of men and women who feel like the writer of that letter. Perhaps there is no subject about which there is so much ignorance as 'The Church'. So we are going to consider it now, and since the writer signed himself

'Inquiring Mind' it is only fair that I ask him and you to do some careful and precise thinking.

'Have you left anyone to carry on your work on earth?' says the archangel Gabriel in the legend, to our Lord as he returns after his earthly life. 'Eleven men' was the reply.

There were eleven men who, echoing Peter's cry 'Thou art the Christ', would state their simple creed in the words 'I believe that Jesus Christ is Lord.'

Now there are some people who say 'Religion is only a matter between me and God.' That may be so in their case. But whatever their religion is, it is most definitely not the Christian religion. Christianity knows nothing of a selfish religion. Christ stressed that again and again. Love of God and love of brethren are inseparable.

A society is necessary for life

There is not one of us who can develop our personality in isolation from everyone else. We are not just born a boy or girl, but French, Turk, Russian or English. That is—from our very birth we are a member of a society. So, too, our Lord saw that if the personality of these eleven men was to be fully developed, if they were to be real Christians, then they must keep alive the truth they affirmed—that Christ was Lord—by incorporating it in a society.

You can see this sort of thing happening every day.

Lord Baden Powell conceived the idea that the youth of Britain could contribute in some striking and effective way to the health and welfare of the nation. But his idea would have come to nothing unless he had found some friends who had the the same idea in their minds, and so the idea found expression in a society—the Boy Scout Movement.

A society is necessary for life.

But a society also preserves truth

So it was, that if this belief of the eleven men that 'Jesus Christ is Lord' was a true one, and if it was to live, then it must find expression in a society of all those down the ages who utter this cry.

So far, then, we have seen that some kind of society was necessary if this belief of the disciples was to have life and if it was to be kept true.

But I want you to consider:

The real nature of the church

We tend to regard the Church simply as a human institution prone to all the failings that characterise any other human society. Sometimes, people think of the Church as 'the one on the corner', 'the one where we were married'. How often people say to me 'I went to your church the other day,' or 'I went to your cathedral'. But I haven't got a church. I never shall have. A church is simply an outward symbol. A church is the place where the family of God meet to worship him.

The Church is not just a collection of individuals who are keen about religion and have decided to form a nice little cosy party to propagate their views. It is not a handful of mystics whose experiences are foolishness to their enemies and mysteries to their friends. It certainly is not a collection of parsons who want to keep an organisation going.

The Church's claim is the greatest ever made in history.

She claims to have been originated by God, to be charged with a divine message—the revelation which God inaugurated and Christ fulfilled.

She claims to be the human instrument or agency through which God purposes to extend this self-revelation to the whole world, and through which he offers men resources of spiritual life that enable them to respond to that revelation and to enter into communion with him. That is the Church's claim, nothing less.

Now you will deny this claim if you merely regard Christ as a great or perhaps the greatest prophet and teacher the world has ever known. But if you have thought over what we have been discussing; if you regard Christ as the divine Son of God; if you have been able to give the Christian answer to the

37

questions, why did he come, why did he die, then you will realise that the founding of this society was just as much part of God's plan for the world as it was to send his son into it.

Will you examine this claim of the Church? Divide it into two for the sake of convenience.

(a) 'The Church claims to be the human agency or instrument through which God purposes to extend the revelation of himself to the whole world.'

Would you and I have ever heard of Christ, would we know the story of his life and death and resurrection if it had not been for the Church? Would we be able to convey the knowledge and effects of this life and death to the world, were it not for the wonderful stories and incidents so simply told and carefully treasured by the Church down the ages? If there had been no Church, no community of people who accepted the risen Jesus as the Christ of God, there would have been no Christian religion.

So we can resolutely affirm the first half of the claim.

What of the second part? (b) 'Through the Church God offers men resources of spiritual life that enable them to respond to the revelation of himself in Christ, and to enter into communion with him.'

This brings us to Pentecost or Whitsunday as we call it.

Whatever may or may not have happened on that day, only one thing matters . . . 'they were all filled with the Holy Ghost.' It is this which made the day one of the landmarks in the history of Christianity. It is this which justifies it being described as the birthday of the Church. Christ had said 'I will not leave you comfortless, I will come to you', and everyone present felt a personal experience of the presence and power of God. They felt bound to God and to one another. They knew that Christ had kept his promise, not to leave them alone.

But that was not all. These members of the early Church realised that this personal influence of the Holy Spirit had far-reaching results. We have all experienced the personal influence of our friends, shown in outward acts, a conversation, a handshake, a kiss. So it was that under the personal influence of the

Holy Spirit certain outward signs and acts came to be associated with the closest communion between the disciple and his Lord. So it was that, in Christian experience, Holy Communion is not the only, but it is the supreme means by which the union of the Christian with Christ is sustained, nourished and increased. Under the forms of bread and wine Christ gives himself to the good companions who are in love and charity with their neighbours.

> Thou who dost give thy very self, Lord Jesus,
> For food to those that seek the things above,
> What less than self-surrender dare I offer
>   Thine awful love?
>
> (George Lefroy)

So then we've reached three conclusions.

(a) Christ founded a Church because it was part of God's original plan for the world that the knowledge of Christ's messiahship should not die but live.

(b) Christ founded a Church so that Chritians down the ages should remain true to their original faith.

(c) Christ founded a Church so that God might entrust to this Church the means of grace whereby the creature might worship the creator, the Christian meet his Lord.

CONCLUSION

So join the other good companions in the district where you live. Your parish church needs you. If your parish church is, as you think, 'dead' it needs your prayers and work and witness to make it come alive.

For the thrilling challenge is that we are the Church. If we liken the Church to a body, then each of us is some part of the body. If we liken the Church to a garden, then we are flowers in that garden; aiding or detracting from its loveliness according to whether our spiritual lives blossom or decay and die.

But, perhaps, like me, you will get the most inspiration if you think of the Church as a building. Other foundations can no man lay than that which had been laid, Jesus Christ our Lord. Down the ages Christians have built on this foundation, each one bringing his particular contribution, the contribution of his life. Difficulties have been overcome, doubts dismissed. Higher and higher the building rises, built with millions of bricks that are Christian lives, and still it is not finished. Past generations have done their work to the glory of God and have handed on to us the sacred trust. For it is a threefold partnership—between those who have gone before, those who are living, and those still to be born.

But the point is—what about you? Are you playing your part?

LENT

How to keep going

On the front page of a Christmas card in 1937 was written:

In 1801 Wilberforce said: 'I dare not marry—the future is so unsettled.' In 1806 William Pitt said: 'There is scarcely anything round us but ruin and despair.' In 1848 Lord Shaftesbury said: 'Nothing can save the British Empire from shipwreck.' In 1849 Disraeli said: 'In industry, commerce and agriculture there is no hope.' In 1852 the dying Duke of Wellington said: 'I thank God I shall be spared from seeing the consummation of ruin that is gathering about us'. Then, inside, the card read: 'So after all we can still wish you a merry Christmas and a happy New Year.'

It all depends on whether you have the power to keep going. This applies most of all to those who are trying to be Christians. You may have set out on the venture of life. You may have determined that God is your objective and that you want to do his will. You may really know and face the snags. You may have joined yourself to others in the Family of God who are trying to build his kingdom here on earth. But have you the power to keep going?

That power comes through prayer.

How shall I pray?

Here is a very simple illustration that has helped me. A small girl is left in the house for the first time while her mother goes to the shops. Like all normal mothers, her last words are: 'Be a good girl while I am out.'

As soon as the door shuts, the girl wanders all over the house trying out the various things that interest her, probably looking at all sorts of things that intrigue her, and turning on one or two taps that usually don't come under her 'sole command'. Eventually she gets bored with this and goes into the kitchen—usually the most exciting room in the house. High up between the mantelpiece and the window is a cupboard which, as she has often been told, is out of bounds. This is just the moment to look inside. She is not very tall. She pushes a chair against the kitchen table, climbs on to the table, opens the cupboard. On the top shelf is a glass jar containing some pink glutinous substance. On tiptoe she reaches up, puts in a finger, takes it out and licks it. It tastes very good. Jelly usually does. In her eagerness to reach it, she overbalances, puts out her hand to save herself falling and with a splintering of glass crashes it through the window-pane. She falls off the table with a scream. Nobody comes. There is nobody to come. She looks at her hand. It is not bleeding. She decides not to cry. Getting the broom, dustpan and brush she sweeps away the offending glass, puts back the chair, closes the cupboard. All is left exactly as it was—except for a gaping hole in the window.

Anxious to get this event out of her mind, she goes out into the garden. There over the fence is her friend from next door looking pretty glum. She inquires why? Her father is in the army and he's just gone abroad. But, much worse still for a small girl, she has lost her sweets which she had carefully hidden away somewhere. Our little girl wishes she could help somehow. It is getting late now, and she wishes that her mother would come back. She hears the gate, and runs to meet her and kisses her.

'I'm so glad you're back', she says.

'Have you been a good girl?' says her mother—the invariable

question on these occasions. She is just about to say 'Oh yes' when into her mind's eye comes the aching void in the window, and she replies ruefully:

'Well I did have a bit of an accident with the kitchen window.'

'Show me', says the mother, and a sorrowful procession winds its way to the kitchen. From the doorway, the mother can see at a glance exactly what has happened. Besides, she has been a little girl herself and knows her daughter too. But her first enquiry is:

'Have you hurt yourself?'

'Oh no.'

'Let me see,' and there follows a careful examination of the offending hand in case there are bits of glass left in it. Then the mother explains just why she had put that cupboard out of bounds, and how the small girl might have done herself real injury. She extracts a promise that she will not offend again. The girl gives it, really meaning what she says.

'Then we'll say no more about it,' says the mother, realising that the little girl has been sufficiently punished already by her fright; and the girl knows she has got away with it far more easily than she really deserves.

'Look what I've brought you from the shops,' says the mother, handing the child something which she knows she likes.

'That's smashing,' says the girl—or whatever word is her brother's latest craze.

'What have you been doing with yourself?' asks the mother. Suddenly the girl remembers her friend next door and asks her mother if she could possibly have some money to buy some sweets for her. Glad that she is beginning to think more about other people, the mother readily consents. To the door the child flies with the money her mother gives her, and just as she is about to go she adds 'And may I get some sweets for myself?' Laughingly the mother consents, knowing that request sounds more like her daughter's normal self.

Now there in that simple story is the whole realm of prayer.

Adoration (the kiss when the mother returns). O God I love thee, help me to love thee more.

Confession (I've had a bit of an accident with the kitchen window). Isn't that exactly how we are tempted to talk? But with God we must be blunt and honest. I've sinned in thought, word and deed, especially this . . . and this . . . and this.

Thanksgiving (the gift from the shops). God I thank thee for the sky above us, the earth beneath our feet, for my home, wife, children, friends. For this that happened today. For help with that interview I was dreading and came off far better than I dared to hope. For this and this and this.

Supplication (the girl next door). Prayers for other people. For your own family, for someone at work who is having a difficult time just now. For your friend who's just been admitted to hospital. And if you don't know how to pray for other people, then you can't do better than you did when you were a child, 'God bless X or Y'. You may not know what is best for them. God does. Perhaps they may need the courage of Christ on the cross to bear suffering. Perhaps they may need the moral strength of Christ to face ridicule. God knows—leave it to him.

Supplication (for myself). All those things about which you want to ask God. But do notice they come last.

A doration
C onfession
T hanksgiving
S upplication
   (i) For others
   (ii) For myself.

So if you just remember the words A C T S it will give you the clue to the pattern in which you can learn to pray.

LENT

Why do men suffer?

Why on earth should it happen to him? What's she done to deserve this? Surely it would be a merciful release if he died? I can't bear to see him suffer.

Pain, suffering, disease. The moment you begin to think at all you've got to face the question—why? Anyone who is trying to live the Christian life has got to face this problem of suffering squarely. Perhaps you know people who really want to try and follow Christ's way of living, but somehow they just can't reconcile Christianity and a God of love with the suffering of someone they love. What will you say to them . . . and to yourself?

That's the great question. 'Why do men suffer . . . why all this pain?' That little boy down the road, happily playing about a few days ago, suddenly struck down with infantile paralysis; that mother of a family taken off to hospital; the young man at the office, and others some of them specially dear to you.

No complete answer

It wouldn't be so hard to understand, would it, if the people who suffered were themselves evil and unpleasant? But so often it seems just the opposite.

'What has Christianity to say about all this?' you ask. 'You Christians talk about a good God. You say that God is like Jesus. Jesus wouldn't want all this suffering to happen . . . I can't understand it.'

Now right at the start I want to say that there isn't a Christian man or woman . . . there isn't a Christian minister of religion who doesn't meet this problem every day of his life . . . He longs to be able to give a complete answer to it. But There is no Complete Answer to it. Do not trust anyone who says there is.

There are some people who attribute all this suffering and evil to the Devil. Oh, I don't mean a peculiar creature with horns and a tail. He's been disposed of long ago by two little girls playing together and one asking the other, 'Do you believe in the Devil?' 'Of course not, silly, it's like Santa Claus, it's only Daddy.'

By a devil these people mean that gigantic power of evil that is apparent to anyone who lives in the world for more than a moment. And yet this doesn't help us to solve the problem.

For either God or the Devil is master. And if a real God, if a good God, why all this suffering? So that answer won't do.

Once again we ask: What has Christianity to say?

Facing facts

Christianity looks facts in the face. Christianity says pain is real.

Christianity faces squarely all the suffering in the world. And Christianity admits there's no slick answer to this problem . . . but before you begin to think about it just come along . . . Come to a green hill outside a city wall. Don't talk for a moment . . . just look. Over there. A man, THE man, Jesus, Son of God, dying by inches on a cross-shaped gibbet; the nails splintering his tendons, the agony on his face, the parched lips . . . There's real pain. There's real suffering. There's no 'fancy' about that. It is cruel, stark, bloody. It's utterly undeserved.

Don't talk . . . just look.

> See from His head, His hands, His feet,
> Sorrow and love flow mingling down,
> Did e'er such love and sorrow meet,
> or thorns compose so rich a crown?
>
> (I. Watts)

Now I believe that the words of that hymn give an insight into the heart of this great problem of suffering.

> Forbid it Lord, that I should boast
> Save in the Cross of Christ my God . . .

And that's exactly what we Christians do. We boast in the Cross. We tell everyone about it. Of course, we don't separate it in our minds from the end of the story, the great news of Easter Day and the Resurrection. But because of the Cross we do know that the God we worship didn't sit, doesn't sit, remote, careless of mankind in some far off comfortable sphere. He came down, he comes down. He is bearing our griefs and carrying

45

our sorrows. He knows all about pain. 'We may not know, we cannot tell what pains He had to bear.' True. And the pains he did bear don't give me a theory about pain. They do help me to bear it.

Suffering shared

Have you ever noticed in a great hospital how each patient seems to share in a fellowship of suffering? Have you ever watched someone's character being softened and refined by suffering—in a most extraordinary way? And of course you've admired the wonderful flood of loving skill and sympathy that flows over the sick and suffering. 'You learn to love people', says a Westminster Hospital nurse, writing of her job. 'You meet pain, suffering and heartache until sometimes the weight of sorrow seems almost unbearable. But in it all, and through it all there emerges such courage, heroism and patience, such cheerfulness, kindliness and gratitude, such forbearance, faith and hope as is seldom seen elsewhere. That is why,' she adds, 'I pray God that he will use me, take my hands, my feet, my heart and my mind so that for his sake, and in his strength I may love and serve his children.'

That's what she wrote. And all this because, faced by the Cross, this nurse and thousands of others in all sorts of jobs are prepared to give their lives to him who suffered to the utmost.

Whose fault?

But that's not all. When a Christian talks about the Cross; when he seems to hear someone asking, 'were you there when they crucified my Lord?' he has the answer, 'Yes.' He was there. So was I. So were you. So was the whole human race. Up there on the cross is man, all humanity gathered up in the Person of the One Man, Jesus. Of his own will and choice he stretches out his hands from his cross and grasps all sin and takes it to himself. Your sins and mine. For he is also God. And with God there is no time. So up there on the cross is every act which has caused your suffering, and the many acts of yours which have caused

46

suffering to others; the few sins of other people that have hit the headlines and about which we have been smug, and the many sins of yours and mine that only we know and are thoroughly ashamed of. And because God so loves the world, he is drowning in the muck and garbage of human sin.

And yet I go on saying that 'sin doesn't matter': that boys will be boys; youth must have its fling; she must have a 'good time' before she settles down. And yet I go on reading that rotten book, keep on with that friendship, play about with temptation. I prattle on about 'little sins' and 'white lies' the 'necessity of business-untruths'. I listen to what the world says about immorality; that it's 'good for you', 'you can't help it', the adulterous are merely 'temperamental'. Yet I still hold back from real and practical repentance. I'm young yet. There's plenty of time. I'm old. I can't make a fresh start now. But the truth is, I won't. I just don't want to enough. I've too much pride.

And yet . . .

> When I survey the wondrous Cross
> On which the Prince of Glory died,
> My richest gain I count but loss
> And pour contempt on all my pride.

CONCLUSION

So then, if you want to begin to see into the mystery of suffering you must stand close to the cross of Christ. There's plenty of room there. There were only three women and one man when he was dying. Look at those outstretched hands, the only hands that can make a silk purse out of a sow's ear. And watch how he dies on the Friday that men call Good. Not in failure, but in triumph, wringing from the hardened officer of the Roman army the heartfelt cry 'Truly this man was the Son of God.' Soon Easter Day will dawn. But till then . . . come. Where? Outside a city wall.

LENT

What does Christianity demand?

What does Christianity demand? Someone asked Christ that. Do you remember? Matthew tells about it in Chapter 19. 16-22:

'And, behold, one came . . . for he had great possessions.'

Then there was that other statement of Christ's also recorded by Matthew in Chapter 10, 32-39:

'Whosoever therefore . . . my sake shall find it.'

What then does Christianity demand? Make it more direct, more personal. What does Christ demand?

(a) First—conversion

A turning of your will towards God. A turning of your whole self away from what you want, towards what God wants for you and from you. 'Conversion'—don't be afraid of the word. It is too rarely used these days. The process may be a sudden one. It sometime is. It was so for a brilliant university graduate called Saul. Bent on persecution, he was struck down in his tracks and faced by the awful nearness of the Most High God. It was so for Pascal, the great writer, when on the day of what he called his 'conversion' he wrote in his diary . . . at the top of the page 'Fire': in the middle of the page 'Joy': at the bottom of the page 'Jesus Christ'. More often it is a gradual process in which intellect, emotion and will go hand in hand; till— almost silently—God has passed under the low lintel of the human heart and we find ourselves at home with him—gladly subject to his will. First, then, Christ demands conversion.

(b) Then follows Repentance

'Woe is me for I am undone; because I am a man of unclean lips and I dwell among a people of unclean lips; for mine eyes have seen the king, the Lord of Hosts.' That's what Isaiah said. But it's not Isaiah now, it's you and I.

Reformation and reconstruction must begin in me before I build a brave new world for God.

And then we're faced with a question. We should like the question simply to be 'Whom do men say that I the Son of Man am?' For in that case we could discuss the issue in a dispassionate, academic sort of way, and, if we felt like it, come to no conclusion. Do you remember how on Calvary when Christ cried out in agony, one person took action and ran and fetched a sponge. The rest said 'Let be'. They were in the majority. They usually are. If a definite decision has to be made, a public figure to be condemned or acclaimed, it is always easier to say 'Let be'—to come to no decision. And if you're clever about it, you call it 'suspending judgement'. Though in your heart of hearts, of course, you'll know it's either mental timidity or moral cowardice. Lots of people adopt that attitude about Christianity. They begin quite honestly by suspending judgement on Christ. If you ask them about their religion they say they can't give an answer as yet. Then one morning late in life they wake up to find that having given no answer to the claims of Christ all this time, they have in fact answered 'No'.

Christ asks you for a decision now.

For, looking at each one of us, he says: 'Whom say ye that I am?'

'If—despite so many doubts—you can humbly begin to say 'Thou art the Christ the Son of the living God,' at once Christ will make demands upon you . . . energetic thinking and decisive action.

Energetic thinking and decisive action

It is worth-while looking at the type of character which Christ admires. How many of the parables turn on energy? The parable of the talents turns on energetic thinking and decisive action. These are the things that Christ admires—in the widow who will have justice:

in the virgins who thought ahead and brought extra oil;
in the vigorous man who found treasure and made sure of it;

in the friend at midnight, who hammered and hammered
and hammered till he got his loaves;
in the man who will hack off his hand to enter into life.

On the other hand, Christ is always against the life of drift,
the half-thought-out-life. There they were, he says, in the days
of Noah, eating, drinking, marrying, dreaming—and the flood
came and destroyed them. There is the person who everlastingly
says and does not do, who promises to work and does not work;
who receives a new idea with enthusiasm but has not enough
depth of nature for it to root itself; who builds on sand—the
sort who compromises, who tries to serve God and Mammon.
No, says Christ, it is energy of mind I ask for—with me or
against me.

And if you are with him you will want to worship.

If you are with him you will want to pray.

If you are with him you will come to see that his death on the
cross was not just a tragic event in history. You begin to understand his cry . . . 'Love I gave thee with myself to love, and thou
must love me who have died for thee.'

Can you say this?

> Just as I am, though tossed about
> With many a conflict, many a doubt;
> Fightings within and fears without,
> Lord of my life, I come.
>
> (Charlotte Elliott)

Conversion, Repentance, Energetic Thinking and Decisive
Action, Worship. Prayer; the acceptance of the cross—these are
some of the things that Christ demands. His call is personal. It
is to each individual; yet set in the context of a family. To each
he says: 'Give me your mind and your heart. Together and step
by step we will win the kingdom; and you shall be sharers in
my joy as you have been in my temptation.'

CONCLUSION

So to the man or woman who asks the question, 'What does

Christianity involve, what does Christ demand?' I say, 'Ally yourself, perhaps for the first time, perhaps with renewed determination, to the family of Christ where you live. If the family is small it needs your support.

If the family is weak it needs your strength.

If the family lacks fire it needs your enthusiasm.

If the family lacks boldness it needs your courage.

If the family lacks vision it needs your prayers.'

In his strength past generations have done their work to God's glory and have handed on the sacred trust to us. It is a partnership between those who have gone before, those who are living and those still to be born.

PALM SUNDAY

No work today

'No work today'. These were the words which began that day in the boy's life which he never forgot. It was early morning, and he had just started to stitch a leather sandal which had been brought in for repairs when his father came down into the little workshop and uttered these magic words, 'no work today'. 'But what about these sandals?' asked the boy. 'The rich merchant is coming for them today.' 'He won't come today', replied his father, 'he'll be at the Judgement Hall listening to the trial. That's where I'm going, and you can come too, if you like.' The boy needed no further invitation, and in a minute father and son were hurrying along by the city wall, past the Damascus Gate, and along to the Praetorium.

It was still early but a huge crowd was already gathered. The boy could pick up scraps of conversation from here and there—stories of arrest, a trial before Herod, sent back to Pilate, accusations of blasphemy, making himself a king, cries of 'death', 'crucify!' and 'away with him'. The boy was mystified, for all around he saw men whom he knew, men who but a few days ago had hailed this prophet of Nazareth and strewn palms in his way. He could not understand this change of heart. Suddenly Pilate himself appeared on the balcony with the prisoner, and the crowd seemed to go mad. Pilate's words were drowned in the uproar, and a shout of 'crucify' filled the air. Pilate seemed to hesitate, and the crowd, urged on by the priests, became more frenzied. The boy was almost swept off his feet and could see nothing more until the crowd must have had its way, for many of them began to run off to the gate of the city so as to get a good position to see the execution. The boy slipped down a side street, and making his way round to the city wall, he climbed up the steps to a little cranny from which he had often watched the camel trains coming to the city. From there he saw everything. He never forgot what he saw. Years afterwards he could see it all as plainly as on that day. The howling mob with the prisoner in the midst, making its slow procession to Golgotha. The three crosses and the strange calmness of the chief prisoner. The ghastly sound as the nails pierced the hands of the condemned men, and the accompanying jeers of the crowd.

As he watched the boy seemed to be able to divide the onlookers into five groups.

First the four people, three women and a man, who stood close to the foot of the Galilean's cross; then the executioners looking to see that their job was well done; further off a little band of men who appeared to be followers of the prophet, and who cast anxious and terrified glances at him over their shoulders. Then the curious mob, not interested in justice or the rights and wrongs of the case, but eager to see the spectacle. And last of all there were those who remained in Jerusalem, whom the boy could see busy at their work, apparently ignorant of the scene that was being enacted outside the city wall.

Five groups

Five different groups, near or far from the Cross.

That was what the boy saw, and what you and I are to see once again this week. We Christians talk much about the cross; it is a question whether we bear it much. The distance in time between the Calvary the boy saw and the one which we see, the familiarity with the thought of the cross, and the certainty of Easter Day to follow, all these have blurred for us its horror and humiliation, its agony and shame.

But even today there are those five groups, near or far from the cross.

Let us look at them in turn.

(1) There are those who remain in the city, who know nothing as yet of Christ, who never heard that he died that they might be forgiven. But don't think that they are only to be found in darkest Africa or India, they are here at hand. Thousands of people in those vast areas springing up around our cities, full of children who simply don't know what happened on Good Friday, because their parents are not quite certain. Dare we neglect this missionary work at our doors?

(2) Then there is the curious mob who see the tragedy unfolded before their eyes but care not for it. It is nothing to them as they pass by. Good Friday—well another bank holiday, another football match. The story of the cross—very interesting. Let us remember how Paul preached at Athens the gospel of Christ crucified and they said: 'That's very interesting, we must hear you again.' Result—no church at Athens! No, the gospel, the good news of Christ is not simply interesting. Men must accept it and be saved, or reject it and face the consequences. That is the challenge.

(3) The executioners. 'Only doing their duty, obeying orders,' you may say. But they typify to us today those people who by their wilful sin add to our Lord's Passion. People who knowingly employ shady methods of business and force others to do so too. People who wilfully misuse their authority over those placed under them, and add to the sufferings of the Lord who died to save us all. If we are one of the executioners we can remember that it was the chief of them who, faced by the cross confessed—'Truly this man was the Son of God.'

(4) But perhaps we feel that though we know these groups, the men who knew nothing about the Passion, the curious sight-seeing mob, and the executioners, yet we ourselves do

not belong to any of those. Then what of the fourth group —the apostles and others who loved Jesus, afar off, casting terrified glances over their shoulders towards him?

Are we in that group? We have been baptised, we have been confirmed. 'O Jesus we have promised to serve Thee to the end' and then that service has meant sacrifice, a cross. We have allowed our prayers to become irregular, we have been ridiculed for going to church, and through lack of preparation our Communions seem useless. Discouraged and ashamed, we cast a backward glance at the Crucified, with arms outstretched, but we look from afar, we dare not draw near. And yet he seems to say: 'But love I gave Thee with Myself to love, and Thou must love Me who have died for Thee'.

So there is still the last group, the smallest of all—the three women and one man—at the foot of the cross. Shall we not try and join those faithful hearts? There the bustle and noise of the world will be eclipsed, and we can offer all the work we have to do to Jesus on the cross, with Jesus on the cross to God. As we read that story written in characters of blood, we repent of our sins and shortcomings, our denials of our Lord, and we resolve that with his help we will stand close to him in his sufferings as we hope to do in his glory. For our nearness to Jesus on the throne in eternity depends upon our nearness to him on the cross in time.

EASTER

Jesus and the resurrection

'What will this babbler say?' (Acts 17.18)

This was the question they asked each other when Paul preached at Athens. They had had their ears tickled by strange doctrines; they had heard tell of strange gods. It was all rather disturbing. So they got hold of him—not violently, of course, for they were respectable Athenians, not vulgar Corinthians, and asked him what it was all about, muttering behind his back . . . 'What will this babbler say?'

His answer . . . 'Jesus and the Resurrection'.

That's why Christianity exists. That's why anyone anywhere has ever built a Christian church. That's why anyone anywhere has ever said the Lord's Prayer. That's why you're listening to these words in a sermon that would be non-existent except for Jesus and the Resurrection.

If on Easter Day a man from Outer Space or a pagan English-man walked in a Christian church, looked at the people, the choir, the cross-shaped gibbet on the altar, the man in the pulpit, and, somewhat bewildered, muttered half aloud: 'What will this babbler say?', everyone from the oldest man to the youngest child should want to get up together and with a mighty crash of organ and bells shout at the top of their voices: 'Jesus and the Resurrection'. What effect would it have? Well, the man from Outer Space and certainly the pagan Englishman would be rather shocked. He might laugh. He might mock. Some of the Athenians did. Others thought it all very interesting and hoped the preacher would come and discuss it at the club one day. Others did the same as when Jesus came to London . . .

> They simply passed Him by.
> They did not touch a hair of Him;
> They merely let Him die.
> For men had grown more tender,
> And would not cause Him pain.
> They only just passed down the street
> And left Him in the rain.
>
> (Studdert Kennedy)

His life

For look how he lived. Born in an obscure village, the child of a peasant woman, living in a working-class home for thirty years. Then wandering about teaching and preaching for three years. During all that time he never travelled two hundred miles from where he was born. During all that time he never spoke to a fraction as many people as Robin Day spoke to in Panorama on Monday night. He never wrote his memoirs. He had no regular column in any paper. That's how he lived.

His death

Look how he died. Never was there so complete a fiasco and failure. Everyone disowned him. They heard him say he was forsaken by God; his friends deserted him, one of them—a suicide—had just sold him for less than £4. His mother's heart was broken; his companions were a couple of half-dead highwaymen; the crows were waiting, the grave ready. He died 'world's vermin pinned to the world's barn door, despised and rejected.' 'Poor little man' said the public as they hurried by the foot of the hill outside the city wall . . . 'perhaps the sentence was unjust . . . but it really doesn't matter . . . it's all over . . . it is finished.'

So would our Christian faith be if Christ's suffering had come to nothing. If he was just one more unfortunate mortal gone to his death, well, that's that. If just another man who's lost the hopeless fight against death, why bother about him?

Easter faith

But the Christian belief, based upon unshakeable evidence, is that Christ rose from the dead. That he is alive for evermore. That's why 'Jesus Christ is risen today' is the shout that sweeps the morning skies around the world on Easter Day.

And remember this. The Resurrection is not an appendage to the Christian faith. It's not tacked on at the end because it will be good 'box office' to have a happy ending. Jesus and the Resurrection *is* the Christian faith. It is its only sufficient basis and guarantee. For all the evidence of the New Testament shows that the core of the good news that spread throughout the world was not: 'Follow this teacher and do your best' . . . 'lead a decent life and do as you would be done by' . . . 'Service above Self' . . . (these are the best set of ethics on record so far) . . . 'Religion is just between a man and his God'. Not at all. The core of the gospel message was, and always will be, JESUS

AND THE RESURRECTION. Take that away and you take away Christianity.

Your response

So you have to accept him or reject him. 'With me or against me?' he asks. There's no 'pending basket' into which the claims of Christ can be put.

Do you accept him? You who lost your husband in the First World War and your son in the second. You who watched your wife die slowly of a dread disease. A car came round the corner, not very fast, but fast enough to kill your child. That chap at the office, just got engaged, killed in a plane crash. Where are they now? What happens after death? Everyone wants to know. Only Christ can give the answer. And because you accept him as Lord of this world and that which is to come you trust him. It's enough for you that he says: 'Today shalt thou be with me in Paradise . . . I am looking after your loved ones for you . . . they are safe and happy with me . . . nothing can my power withstand.' That is what Easter Day says to you.

And you who are just an ordinary person trying to live a Christian life in your job and your home. You know well enough that we still sin and suffer; there is still adultery, gossip, scandal, cruelty and lies. Yet every time you pray to God, every time you make an act of real penitence, every time you resist the temptation to what you try and pretend are little sins, white lies, business untruths; every time you turn your back on the temptations that you hope nobody knows about except you and God, then, because of Easter Day, you and countless Christians share a victory which death itself cannot defeat.Why?

Jesus and the Resurrection.

EASTER

Three texts

The first day of the week cometh . . . So they ran both together . . . Stooping down and looking in . . . (John 20.1, 4, 5)

The first day of the week cometh

Who? . . . Oh yes, it was Mary Magdalene. Someone who had been a prostitute, met Jesus, and became a saint. And now . . . the first day of the week cometh . . . who? . . . well you! When? She came early . . . she wanted to meet her Lord. Did you come early? Did you—as some say—'go to early' this morning? Did you fulfil your obligation as a member of the Church of England to make your communion on Easter Day—unless age or sickness hinder you?

And your worship? It's no good really, is it, arguing as to whether the Sabbath and the Christian Sunday mean the same thing? 'Remember to keep Holy the Sabbath day . . .' is quite clear in its meaning, isn't it? It means that though you work hard during the week, the first and vital thing on Sunday is to worship God. A game of golf, by all means; a wonderful walk or drive, by all means; but first, without any shadow of doubt, without any complaints about distance, or time or place, or the parson . . . the worship of God, your bounden duty. What about the future? Make a resolution now.

They ran both together

She had fallen in love with him three and a half years ago. She had been faithful to him while he had been abroad for two years. She had not been impatient when he found it difficult to settle down after his return. Now they were expecting to get engaged. 'I want to ask you something, vicar', she said, 'do you think it is ever possible for a husband and wife to be really happy if one has no religion? You see, he says it doesn't mean a thing to him; and he won't even have any instruction.'

Can one run alone, mustn't both run together? Was that your son? Do you blame her for breaking it off? For to her Christ is alive, to him he doesn't exist.

Said a young mother the other day to a Christian psychiatrist . . . 'What should parents teach their children about religion if they have no beliefs themselves?' Said the psychiatrist, 'You can't lead a child further than you've gone yourself . . . it's no good pretending that he won't sense your own doubts . . . you've got to resolve those first if you want to pass on to your children something real' . . . they both ran together.

Perhaps you're a bit out of training in meeting Christ. Perhaps you haven't made many journeys to see him this last year. Perhaps on each of the Church Festivals you don't run to meet him, but at any rate you let your family or your friends, or some forgotten echo of early habit or custom or training take you to church. But what of the future? You and your wife, you and your son, you and your husband, daughter, must run together. Make a resolve now.

But perhaps you're here without someone you love, because they are in paradise. Perhaps you have always done everything together. Remember that just because of Easter Day you are still together, together on the road that is the work and will of God. Go forward, and may Easter peace be yours.

The first day of the week.

They ran both together.

Stooping down and looking in

Yes, that's the condition. You won't find him if you're proud; you can't meet him as man to man, because it's man and God. He came down low for you, and died a bloody death, so at least surely you can stoop. Not absurdly low, low enough to kneel, low enough to put out your hands, low enough to hear him say, 'Take eat, this is my body, this is my blood which is given for you' . . . yes for you, despite all I know about you, despite all the world knows about you, despite all that you think nobody knows about you but yourself . . . I believe in you, I died for you . . . and now I am alive for evermore. So come humbly to my table, as they did to my tomb; stoop down, it may break your pride, you must risk that; it may mean giving up that secret vice, you must face that . . . it may mean making your religion live again after years of respectable lip-service . . . you must prepare for that.

For the message of Easter Day is Jesus and the Resurrection.

This is the unique claim of Christianity. This is the truth that swept this morning's stars from the sky ... Jesus and the Resurrection.

That is why today ... the first day of the week ... came Mary and you, and millions throughout the world. That is why you and others must run together. That is why all must stoop down, look in and, finding the tomb empty, find Christ alive, now and for evermore.

EASTER

Our witness

'This Jesus God raised up, and of that we are all witnesses.' (Acts 2.32)

INTRODUCTION

Have you read Graham Greene's novel *The Comedians*? It is essentially about the meaning of commitment. It is set in Haiti.

One of the characters in the novel is a dedicated Communist being hunted by the secret police of the Dictator, who knows that he will be murdered. He leaves a letter written to a Catholic friend, to explain what has happened should he disappear. In the course of it he writes: 'It must be admitted that in the past both the Catholic Church and the Communist Party have committed many terrible crimes. Nevertheless I believe it is better to have blood on your hands than water—like Pilate!'

Commitment divisive

A religious faith, a commitment either to a personal God or to an ideology is always divisive. Religious faith, whenever it is more than a merely formal adherence to a code or a tradition, immediately separates man from man. It separates a group from the mass. It separates those who believe from those who do not.

'This Jesus God raised up, and of that we are all witnesses.' Are we? Do *you* believe that? Many don't.

Listen. Procula, Pilate's wife, is speaking. She is asking the Officer in charge of the execution: 'Do you think he is dead?'

'No, lady, I don't.'

'Then where is he?'

'Let loose in the world, lady, where neither Roman nor Jew can touch him. Let loose from the limitations of the flesh, alive for evermore, King Eternal, Judge of the whole earth.'

(Winifred Taylor)

Do you believe that? Many don't.

Jesus Christ is risen today. That mighty act of God is why we are here today. 'Christ is risen' proclaims an act of God which is a miracle. There is a no non-miraculous Christianity. If you cannot accept a miracle you cannot accept Jesus and the Resurrection.

Yes, there are other religions which make no such claim. Buddhism is one. The founder was an Indian Prince who lived a noble life, founded a monastic order, was seen to die by his disciples, and dying, bade them remember his teaching. Islam is another world religion, founded by a Prophet and leader of men who claimed to speak for God, and whose sayings are preserved in the Moslem Bible. But the Early Church's claim is our claim—'Jesus and the Resurrection'.

Of course such an amazing claim is divisive. Didn't Christ warn us? 'Suppose ye that I am come to give peace on earth? I tell you nay, but rather division: for henceforth there shall be five in one house divided, three against two and two against three.'

Yes, the Resurrection separates those who believe and those who do not. It is a call to commitment. It is a call to separation.

No easy task

How does that touch you? Remember the response is to the person of Christ, then to the faith he proclaims. If that is true, and Christ said it was, it is as true for Surrey as it is for Saigon. It is as true for Harlem as it is for Mayfair. It is as true for Peter and James and John as it is for you and you and you.

What does all this involve?

Can you have a better approach or a more religious approach to life's problems than that? And as a Christian, a committed Christian, you do not imagine it will be easy. For it is, perhaps, easy to be an idealist provided you never have to make decisions or take action.

It is, perhaps, easy to be a consistent pragmatist provided you don't look too closely at your own motives or compulsions.

But we who are witnesses to the Jesus whom God raised up have to keep our ideals bright and shining in spite of the disillusionment of human existence: in spite of the constant current attempts to denigrate the eternal values that Christ proclaimed in word and deed: in spite of the attempt to erode the standards that have been mirrored in the Son of God and caricatured in so many sons of modern man.

It is because our own faith has been dim, apologetic, tentative that Jesus and the Resurrection has found such feeble witnesses.

APPLICATION

I believe that men of faith and their Churches have to proclaim that faith in the plainest possible terms.

Tell the world that the risen Christ demands their intellect, research, thought, wonderings, the kindling of their best imagination.

Tell the world that they must use every available means of communication—press, T.V., drama, music—positively to increase an understanding of human dignity rather than to destroy and diminish it.

Tell the world that the virtues of truth, compassion, chastity, reverence are not outmoded mumblings of elderly fools but true reflections of the Christ who rose and whom to serve is to reign.

Tell the world, yes, tell the world . . . whose world? . . . your world . . . the world where you live . . . the world where you work . . . the children you have . . . the people you influence . . . the public opinion you help to form . . . that you yourself are a witness to the Resurrection of this Christ.

It is always easy to wash one's hands of so desperately personal a responsibility as the proclamation of so dynamic and yet so difficult a gospel. It is easier to wash one's hands than to soil them with the blood of the struggle. It is easier. But it is also fatal. It is the death, not of God, but of man.

'Do you remember the incident of the carpenter?' says the ex-Army Officer to his old friend Pontius Pilate as they reminisce long after their retirement. 'Do you remember the carpenter?... He came from Nazareth. His name was Jesus. You had to have him crucified. Do you remember him, Pilate?'

'Jesus', answered Pilate, 'Jesus of Nazareth. No, I cannot call him to mind.'   (Anatole France)

But *you* can. He is risen. And of all his witnesses *one* is *you*.

HARVEST

INTRODUCTION

I want you to use your imagination. I want you to imagine that at this moment every single church in every single parish in England is having its Harvest Thanksgiving. Sheaves of corn are lying against pillars in the country; fishing nets and crab pots are hung aloft in villages by the sea, glorious flowers decorate a thousand aisles; mammoth loaves and homely marrows sprawl over the window sills and steps of England's churches.

To fill these churches for Harvest Thanksgiving large crowds throng. Countrymen and townsmen, fishermen and dustmen, old and young—all love to see the decorations, to sing the Harvest hymns . . . 'yes, of course, they're going to Harvest Festival round at the church'.

So in the eye of your imagination I want you to see row upon row of English people sitting in the pews of their English churches.

And then, at a given moment, by some strange and mysterious power you are able to read in one all-embracing glance the thoughts of their minds, the very secrets of their hearts, the object of their hopes and dreams. Somewhat to your surprise all these thousands of people fall quite clearly into three groups.

Three groups in church

(1) The *first* consists of those who are instructed and convinced Churchmen and women. They love their church. They will work for it, give of their substance, sacrifice much for it, will gladly live and die in this the church of their Baptism.

There are some of those here today; I know.

(2) Then there is the *second* group. They make their Communion occasionally, come to church from time to time . . . in fact more often than not; and contribute in very careful moderation to the funds of the church, without bothering to acquaint themselves in the slightest degree as to how the money is spent, or whether they are giving anything approaching their fair share.

They are highly critical of the way the church is run, especially of their own clergyman whom, of course, they have a perfect right to criticise. They lead fairly good lives and think the Church is a good agency for teaching sound morals. Any change in the presentation of the faith is suspect. What was good enough for their fathers is good enough for them. If someone asked them what it involved being a member of the Church of England, what you have to do, they would be hard put to it to say . . . and they certainly would not go through the necessary intellectual activity to find out. Their supreme horror is to be thought narrow by their friends; and therefore they cling to a comforting vagueness in all matters of doctrine and discipline. Especially do they hide in vagueness when the Church is so uncomfortably firm about what our Lord did and what he did not teach about marriage.

But when all is said and done they regard themselves as members of the Church of England and if those in the first group, together with us clergy, are sufficiently instructed and enthusiastic, many of these latter will become fine active and informed Christians if we are to win them.

I have reason to think that these are not lacking in this parish.

(3) Then there is the *third* group. They know absolutely nothing about the doctrine and discipline of the Church. They

rarely attend its services except on Harvest Festival, or ... if they're sufficiently frightened ... a day of national prayer. They expect the parson to baptise their children without asking awkward questions; they expect to be married in the church, and they expect to be buried decently ... which to them means with 'benefit of clergy'. They are in all classes of our community; they unhesitatingly describe themselves as 'C. of E.' and would be furious if any attempt was made to unchurch them. Some say, like Burge in Shaw's *Back to Methusalah*: 'The Church is all right essentially; get rid of the bishops; get rid of the candlesticks; get rid of the 39 Articles; and the Church of England is just as good as any other Church; and I don't care who hears me say so.' Others say: 'C. of E.'? of *course* I am. Why I went to the church school, was married in St S— and christened there ... been St S— all m'life and m'father before me ... why I remember ... ' and there follows a flow of reminiscences which have a mighty crescendo until it dawns upon the speaker that the parson is just about to ask when last this keen St S—ite darkened its doors.

Are there some of these in this parish? You know. So does God.

There they are, then, those three quite distinct groups in every parish in the land, sitting in their churches on Harvest Festival.

'Well', you say, 'what about it?' What about it ... ? You've committed yourself three times in this service alone. 'Thy kingdom come ... ' you've said ... I want all men and women to come into the sphere wherein Christ's authority, Christ's standards, Christ's demands are paramount. And if *I* want this *I* must be the first. If I really want a harvest of souls to be gathered by the Lord of the Harvest, then I'd better begin with myself. If I want all those in the third and second groups to come into the first, to learn to know and love our Lord then it's up to me first. How?

APPLICATION

(1) *For a parson:* I must preach the gospel of Christ boldly ...

no watering down to suit modern slackness. I must preach not what man ought to do about God but what God, Almighty, Holy Eternal, Infinite, demands of man. I must proclaim the majesty, the Holiness and Love of God and then, reflected in that burning light, man will come to see himself as he really is and to look for his salvation.

(2) *For a layman and woman:* I must ask myself: 'Do I really know what church membership involves—communion, prayer, bible-reading, alms-giving, self examination, self discipline? The school I'm sending my boy or girl to. Have I really found out how, when and by whom he will be taught about Christ? What sort of example do I set him of worship, prayer and communion? Can I give a simple yet quite definite answer to someone who asks me what Christianity has to say about the great problems that affect daily life, death, disease, marriage, personal relationships, money, self-control?'

In short in which of these three groups am I on this Harvest Festival Sunday?

You know.

So does God.

ALL SAINTS DAY

The mark of a saint

'*Who knoweth whether thou art come into the kingdom for such a time as this?*' (Esther 4.14)

The mark of a saint is consecration not perfection; not a man without faults but a man dedicated to God.

That means you.

INTRODUCTION

When Queen Esther learnt that Mordecai was sad she was distressed. He was her foster-father. To him she owed every-thing. She learnt the cause of his grief—the murderous decree that every Jew should be butchered. As if to turn his mourning into joy by gilding sackcloth, she sends him a new cope, thinking perhaps in womanly fashion that new vestments can mend an aching heart. 'Cannot my conscience thus be eased', she whispers.

To her in return Mordecai sends a copy of the decree itself, that her eyes may see and her heart stir. But still she hopes to be released from the responsibilities of her office and the allegiance of her race. She shelters behind the letter of the law . . . no one may have audience of the king except he be bidden . . . to me the golden sceptre has not beckoned . . . 'cannot my conscience thus be eased', she whispers again. No! Direct and swift comes the answer. 'If thou altogether holdest thy peace at this time, then shall enlargement and deliverance arise to the Jews from another place, and who knoweth whether thou art come into the kingdom for such a time as this?'

Thus challenged she rises to her true stature . . . 'Go, gather together all the Jews that are present in Shushan, and fast ye for me, and neither eat nor drink three days night or day; I also and my maidens will fast likewise; and so will I go in unto the king, which is not according to the law; and if I perish, I perish.'

A fine story with little religious content, says one commentator.

Esther was not dedicated to our God, says another. But *you* are—says your conscience—and who knoweth whether thou art come into the kingdom for such a time as this?

The challenge of the saints

It is All Saints-tide. Rightly and thankfully we give glory to God for all those who have been shining lights in the world in their generation.

Mindful of their example we remember with shame the times when we modern Christians have thought to heal the sickness of our own soul or of our nation with aesthetic delights, beautiful music, fine poetry, great art. But our conscience has said 'no'. In vain we've tried to cuddle our favourite sins and wrap tight about us our pride, precious as a cloth of gold. But truth, as a red hot spear burns through our pride, beats us to our knees, and we admit . . . we have sinned in thought, word and deed . . . and then . . .

Then we are absolved, we rise and hear a voice . . . who knoweth whether thou art come into the kingdom for such a time as this?

The challenge to each of us

Mordecai sends Esther a copy of the decree that brings murder to her race. Surely that will stir her? Does it? Is it *her* affair? Must she take note of the headlines? Look at yours—

Growing tension in the Middle East.

Death sentence on former premier.

Dock Strike Inquiry.

Prison guards held as hostages.

Schoolgirl murdered after party.

Is it your affair? To you the golden sceptre has not beckoned.

You have eaten the bread of heaven, Christ Jesus. You have prayed that your mind may lay hold on what your mouth has received. You bear the full responsibility that three-quarters of the world's population have not had a square meal in the last twenty-four hours. You are responsible that the Christian witness among the whites in South Africa, who came from here, is so weak. You are responsible that polite humanism and good fellowship are accepted as Christianity all around us in this country; and you are responsible that the Christian heritage which inspired the saints and which we enjoy is an unknown thing to the vast majority of our fellow countrymen.

Our part

Make no mistake. I do not **advocate** some neat little plan or tidy solution. Nor is it strident clamour that is needed but informed prayer.

Whether God has allowed us to see our fellow Christians suffering in many parts of the world, or whether the field of pain that we survey is circumscribed, let us pray for the healing of the nations and that, following the example of the saints, we may be shown our part.

For the mark of a saint is consecration not perfection; not a man without faults but a man dedicated to God. That means you . . . and who knoweth whether you are come into the kingdom for such a time as this?

Part Two. Portraits from Old and New Testament

AMOS

The man with a message

INTRODUCTION

There was a total eclipse of the sun. It was the year 763 BC. The kingdom of Israel was divided, southern and northern.

There had been long wars. The northern kingdom found its chief adversary Syria weak, and settled down to enjoy prosperity. But this prosperity only benefited the ruling classes and gave them arrogant self-confidence. Wealth had become unevenly distributed. The law courts were corrupt. The conception of God, the righteous judge, the true God, had faded from the minds of those who wanted no awkward questions asked.

On to this stage came Amos. Other prophets made short utterances, collected and amplified and written down at a later date. But Amos's book is so vivid and original that it is quite clear that it was written down by Amos himself, or by a scribe at his dictation. He has been called the first writing prophet.

Impelled by God to come from the southern kingdom, he was sickened by the catch phrase on everyone's lips when any complaints were made about public immorality or double dealing . . . the day of the Lord . . . the day of the Lord . . . it'll come all right one day . . . when our ship comes home . . . wait and see . . . *laissez faire* . . . don't get excited.

His message

Amos proclaims that God is the God of the whole earth. He made the stars and directs the course of nature and of history.

God is righteous and demands righteousness. He will not grant licence to his favourites as Israel supposes. Righteousness means right dealing in business and everyday life. Justice is judged by this God who judges impartially between man and man without fear or favour.

And whereas others could only see the great day of the Lord as the wished-for fulfilment of all their hopes, Amos could see the lights going out all over Israel and double dealing and national selfishness meeting its just reward.

'The day of the Lord, the day of the Lord . . . ' Yes, says Amos, there will be a day of the Lord . . . it will be darkness and not light. It will be disaster for a single nation. Only national repentance, which means the repentance of people, will save you from our God who is a consuming fire.

Reaction to his message

You will not be surprised therefore that Amos was not popular. A countryman himself, how much he would have preferred to have stayed with his sycamore trees. But God's call must be obeyed. He makes his way to the north; he enters the chapel royal and tells out his message from God. The Lord Chamberlain is scandalised. 'You can't prophesy here, this is the king's court . . . run along back to Judah, and amuse yourself with your mouthings there.'

Then I see Amos drawing himself to his full height. 'I am not an ecclesiastic. I am not some revivalist come from a strange country to seek publicity. I am a respected country farmer where I come from. There it was that God called me. There it was that he laid his hand upon me. There it was that he charged me to speak. I can do no other. For better for worse, though I forfeit my life I must tell you what God has told me to speak. Outward shows and national days of prayer are not enough. You can't escape God though you climb into the heavens or dig down to hell. Our God searches the hearts, from him no secrets are hid. There *will* be a day of the Lord . . . a judgement day . . . and, if you continue as you are doing . . . it will be darkness not light.'

The prophets of repentance have never been popular. John the Baptist ended up in prison. Dean Inge, foretelling almost exactly the plight of England whether she won or lost the first war, earned the nickname of 'the gloomy Dean'. Any priest who, according to his ordination vow, boldly rebukes vice will never have a great following. It is just the same in lay life. Examine your own experience and see. It is by those who are prepared to tell out fearlessly what they know to be God's will; those who are prepared to stand resolutely by God's standards that the kingdom of God is built. By their efforts it is enlarged. It is them of whom God says, 'they shall be mine what time I make up my jewels'.

Amos's cry was 'The day of the Lord' . . . it would be a day of judgement. Men would be judged by a righteous God. He was right. Judgement day will come. You and I will be judged. But next Friday comes first. There's always a next Friday—the day he died. Then we are judged. Not by a triumphant sovereign but by a figure on a cross. So what think you of Christ?

EZRA

The man who looked forward

'And Ezra stood upon a pulpit of wood' (Nehemiah 8.4)

INTRODUCTION

Nehemiah was engaged in rebuilding the city of Jerusalem. The city was wide and large, but the people were few because there was so little accommodation.

Like all great leaders, Nehemiah wanted to know exactly what was the size of the problem. So he held a meeting of the heads of the people.

Meanwhile Ezra, the scribe, is sent to King Artaxerxes in about 400 BC to restore the neglected Law in Jerusalem. Building operations have gone on apace and when Ezra arrives seven months later the whole of the population is gathered together in one place—42,360 of them.

Then, please note, there is a short verse which says much. 'And some from among the heads of Fathers' houses gave unto the work . . . ' i.e. the men visitors pledging themselves before the campaign begins. There follows the account of alms-giving and the amounts which were pledged in this early stewardship campaign to forward this great religious and civic building programme.

Picture the scene then. All this vast concourse is gathered together by the water gate: the people in the centre; in the front the mixed choir; behind the servants; further back at the well the herds and flocks grazing.

It is early morning. The men and women are resting on the ground; for there is no cathedral organist to uplift them with great music before the service begins.

They call upon Ezra, the scribe, to read the Book of the Law. 'And Ezra the scribe stood upon a pulpit of wood.' As he opened the Book of the Law, all the people stood up, as we might stand for the Gospel procession. He reads out distinctly, proud of his privilege as every Reader ought to be: the message is relayed, passed on from mouth to mouth and interpreted, so that the people may understand what is written.

As they listen, memories flood back. There has been an exile and a return . . . Post-exilic reconstruction is sweeping away the old; foundations are obscure; soundings are fashionable; the new is all the vogue. Past failures and absent faces come to mind with the many might-have-beens that dog the thoughts of the old and middle-aged. There are tears in many eyes, courage changing from little to less, and the heart's disgrace in its own ugliness.

But Nehemiah, the national hero, leapt up to join Ezra on his wooden pulpit and called to the people: 'This day is holy unto the Lord, mourn not, nor weep, neither be ye grieved: for the joy of the Lord is your strength.' And all the people went their way to eat and drink and to make great mirth, because they understood that the Law was not to condemn but to guide and encourage. The joy of the Lord is your strength . . . that was the message for which Ezra climbed his pulpit of wood.

A joyful message

That must be the message of anyone who is privileged to preach. Let it ring out from everyone of us in the pulpit. Let those of us who are ordained to minister the word and sacraments note that it is good tidings of great joy which we are commissioned to bring . . . the joy of the Lord is your strength.

I am sick and tired of the black crape-hangers, aren't you? Sick and tired of the 'God is dead' folk, aren't you? Sick and tired of the gaiter-prickers and cassock-clingers, who tempt us to drown our sorrows in the sterile stagnation of dismal despondency. Oh, I know there is cause for anxiety in the world today. There always has been and always will be. Listen: 'Religion is dead; morals are slack; family life is breaking up; social injustice is rife; the clergy are spiritually dead, their ministrations bore them; while the laity are unwilling to support a priesthood who have sunk so low. Worship of God—a pasttime for fools and elderly.'

Which modern newspaper wrote that? None. It was written 398 years before Christ when Ezra's near contemporary, Malachi, describes the prevailing tones of his day. His remedy: . . . 'They that feared the Lord spake one with another . . . and they shall be mine saith the Lord of hosts in the day wherein I make up my jewels' !

Of course, there are terrible hazards in our pathway—sin, selfishness, cruelty of man and the destructive power of the bomb. But we are here as a Christian family and we are here as Christian individuals to acknowledge that there are so many causes for thanksgiving, public and private, that we cannot but shout with the psalmist: 'This is the day that the Lord hath made: I will rejoice and be glad in it . . .'

> To be alive in such an age,
> To live in it! To *give* in it!

74

Give thanks with all thy flaming heart,
Crave but to have in it a part,
Give thanks and clasp thy heritage—
To be *alive* in such an age!

Grounds for Christian optimism

And what, you may ask, are your grounds for this Christian optimism? May I offer you three?

1. A decrease in prejudice.
2. An increase in unity.
3. A new concern for Mission.

(1) *A decrease in prejudice.* I believe our middle-aged generation is less prejudiced than our fathers; while our teenagers are certainly less so than us. Better education, increased travel, wider communication and clearer vision all contribute.

Our gentler attitude to the non-Christian religions is an example. No longer do we approach the heathen in his blindness in a superior know-it-all fashion. We come to him with respect for his religion and culture and with the gift of Christ, who is already his own inner light, who has already shone in his heart. We know that Christ's will is not to destroy his civilisation but to fulfil it, to bring out all its latent goodness and to add to its treasures of mind and spirit to the glory of Christ's Kingdom.

We are beginning to rise above the barriers of race and colour. True, there are from time to time harsh words around the conference tables. But they are words not spears.

Yes, we still have far to go. There are still too many people in this little island who are prone, from a plinth in Trafalgar Square, to talk about the mote of apartheid in South Africa's eye, while completely oblivious of the beam in their own English eye which until all too recently allowed hideous little notices to proclaim: 'Rooms to let: sorry, no coloureds'.

Yes, we have far to go. But the day of the Good Samaritan is with us. None of us can pass the wounded man in the ditch without, at least, a stab of conscience.

A decrease in prejudice.

(2) *An increase in unity.* Today there are some, both within and outside our own communion, who lag behind and try to defend the old Maginot line of sectarianism; some even who still drool the antiquated terms of 'high' and 'low' Church in our own borders; but in the main our generation is for union within the Christian family.

We live in an entirely new world of Christian brotherhood. Understanding and reconciliation are in the very air we breathe. The walls of partition are crumbling before our eyes. Remember they are man-made walls. They have nothing to do with the will of God, with the Gospel of Christ, or the Church which he gave us.

(3) *A new concern for Mission.* In our world we live in one street. Rhodesia, Nigeria and Vietnam are next door. We are close enough to suffer together. 'Who is weak and I am not weak? Who is offended and I burn not?'

Most people want to do something about this concern. We are deeply concerned to share our treasures of spirit and mind and field and factory with all God's children; and we shall welcome the treasures they undoubtedly have for us. This is God's message of interdependence for the nineteen seventies.

Your pulpit

But come back to Ezra. Notice how he stood above the people. He was in the pulpit. There was no hiding him. For you the pulpit is probably not the same shape as it is for a parson. But yours, like Ezra's, is probably of wood. Your office desk, your kitchen table, your bureau, your school desk, the floor of your hospital ward, the barn of your harvest . . . all these places are where you are in full view.

At times you are aware that people are watching you, that they are expecting you to uphold the standards of Christian living and Christian behaviour, of discouraging prejudice, of encouraging unity, of showing concern for mission. At times they turn to you, because you are known to be a priest or a choirman or a churchman or a Christian business man, or a Christian housewife.

But much more often you are watched unawares. A door

opens and you are busy perhaps in conversation with a business equal or inferior. Perhaps the kitchen door is open and you are talking to a tradesman; or the teenage children are hearing you making or breaking your marriage vows. Then people are hearing you preach without your knowing it; they are listening to what you have to say, how you treat your juniors, how you get on with your tradesmen and those who serve you; they know whether the joy of the Lord is your strength.

So go back now to your pulpit of wood wherever it may be. The joy of the Lord is your strength.

MARY MAGDALENE

The woman with a past

Mary Magdalene suffered from a bad past. It dogged her conscience. Then she met Christ face to face—the woman of the streets and the Son of God. There he is, being entertained by Simon, the Pharisee, whose heart is as cold as his welcome. To right the wrong comes Mary with the bad past, her precious burden clasped to her breast—perhaps the costly payment of some lover—the coldness of the Pharisee's welcome warmed and shamed by the glowing fervour of her heart and eye. Her tears contrast strangely with the reserve of the respectable Pharisee.

Silence, orchestrated only by the sobs of a broken and contrite heart.

Mary with the bad past and the Son of God. She sinned much. But she loved much. Christ forgave her much. She followed to the end—and after.

In the garden

She was alone in the garden. Even his dear body was gone. How could she pray with a broken heart? 'They have taken away my Lord . . .' Then he spoke her name . . . it was his voice. Overwhelmed, she falls at his feet in adoration. Can she stay and be alone with him, drinking deep of the grateful springs that well from her heart? But he draws away. He speaks. 'Touch me not. Touch me not but go and say to my brethren . . . I ascend.'

A bad past

You have a bad past. We all have. God knows all about the sins that we hide from the world and even from those we love the most. More respectable sins, you think, than Mary Magdalene's? Who said so? Christ didn't.

But at times, at your confirmation, your first communion, on your wedding day or some anniversary, you really felt that your past was behind you; you really did intend to follow him. And then . . . well, you know . . . they all forsook him and fled. So have you. So have we all. What brought you back? A person? Your conscience? A friend? Then religion got difficult again . . . I used to pray—I don't now . . . they have taken away my Lord. Then perhaps quite unexpectedly he speaks your name, the name he is weaving in your life. It's all right now. It's easy to be a Christian now. Can't you just stay where you are, preferably in church, while you feel like you do and leave your religion at the door and pick it up with a hymn-book next Sunday? But listen . . . He speaks . . .

Touch me not but go

Touch me not. That's what he said to Mary Magdalene. But to you it's different. 'This is my Body . . . take eat and feed on me by faith with thanksgiving.' Thanksgiving . . . how? Go. Go and say. 'Go and say to my brethren . . . I ascend.' Who is he talking to? Every one of us. You with the bad past whom he has forgiven. You who have learnt to love him a little. You who want to touch him at the altar rail and then to keep your religion to yourself. You who think you are too old, too young, too shy, too busy.

His brethren

It'd be easier if he'd send us out on some dramatic mission. After all, Patrick went to Ireland, Columba to Scotland, Wesley all over England. Coley Patterson went to Melanesia. Paul careered all over the place. But wait a minute. Did he? What are the facts? 'Arise and go into the city . . .' where he'd come from; where he was only too well known; where he'd made a fool of himself. And he'd go to start again there and tell his friends how to do the same.

So will you go to Christ's brethren, the people you meet at home, at the office, in your factory? Some may hardly know his name except when someone swears. Will you tell them he is alive, ascended, mighty to save? You'll have to win their friendship. He won yours. It's an old story, but ever new.

'Is there one special thing you'd like to do before you die?' asked Wilfred Pickles of an old Chelsea Pensioner on one of those 'Have a Go' Programmes on the B.B.C.

There was a long pause. Then an old shaky voice said: 'Yes, I'd like to win one soul for Jesus Christ.'

MOTHER AND SONS

'Are ye able?' 'We are able.' 'Ye shall!' (Matthew 20.22)

Mother *can* be so embarrassing.

'Of course she means well, but really!' It is the two brothers who are talking, James and John, sons of Zebedee.

Of course everyone knew Mrs Zebedee, she kept the pub by the side of the lake. She had a word for everyone, ran her place efficiently, and was not too bad. But if you got on the wrong side of her, well her tongue had as rough an edge as anyone's. And heaven help you if you found fault with her two boys, her precious James and John. A lioness with her cubs would be tamer than Mrs Zebedee roused to defend her own.

Actually it was amazing how little spoilt the boys were. John quiet, always a thinker, always saying little, missing little. James more active, a bit of an organiser. Both put up with their mother's unashamed championship.

They all knew Jesus of Nazareth well. They'd heard him

speaking to the crowd by the lake; they'd listened too. They'd done some pretty hard thinking during the night watches. When the call came, they couldn't resist, any more than Peter. They were partners with Simon Peter and Andrew. Together they used to catch fish. Together they'd now try to catch men.

What wonderful times had followed. There'd been other times too; times when people said they were mad; times when people said that the man from Nazareth would end up in prison; times when the authorities looked pretty angry.

Then there were other times, when he healed hundreds who came to him; when he talked to them, his friends—those were the times that could never be described for never man spake as this man.

But Mrs Zebedee was troubled. This Jesus was obviously a great man, a coming man. He was always talking about his kingdom. Of course, *she* couldn't hope for much, she was no better than the rest of the people round about, she wouldn't set herself up to be anyone. But her James and her John, that was different. So if there's going to be any kingdom, if there are going to be any thrones, then her James and her John had better be on them.

'Then came to him the mother . . .' (Matthew 20.20)

'Ye know not what ye ask.' He didn't look at Mrs Zebedee. He summed up the situation. He knew how embarrassed the boys were. He knew that they didn't want to hurt their mother. He had a mother too. So he looked straight at them:

'Are ye able?' 'We are able.' 'Ye shall.'

Do you know what you are in for? Are you prepared to be unpopular, to be thought tame and pious and religious, and 'stuffy'—because you have standards and are prepared to stand by them?

'Are you able to stand by me when things are going against us, when the cry is "not this man but Barabbas"? Are you? You are? You shall . . . but the rewards are not in my hands.'

APPLICATION

Well, what about you? For you see it's to you he's talking. It's no good your mother pleading your cause. He won't mind whether you've been to a good school or a famous school, or who your father or mother is, or whether they've always sent you to church, or whether you've never had any trouble in your family. He'll simply look at you . . .

Are *you* able to follow me?

Have *you* the courage to continue mine for ever?

Do you want to be *confirmed*, made strong, so that you can be loyal?

Are you ready for sacrifice?

Will you follow me and not count the cost?

You will?

You shall . . . but remember you've promised. But you'll keep your promise won't you, week by week, you'll renew it as my guest, here at my table?

You will?

The rewards are not in my hands.

Are you able?

We are able.

Ye shall.

Part Three. Sermons for Special Occasions

CHURCH PARADE OF GUIDES, SCOUTS, ETC.

The Golden Hind, the Christian's badge, the question

Many years ago a little ship put out from Plymouth, bound on a great adventure. The *Pelican* was her name, soon to be changed to the *Golden Hind*, a name more fitting her magical adventures.

On the first morning out to sea, the captain told the bo'sun to pipe all hands on deck, and when they had mustered, he addressed the crew. He made no long speech. That was not the way of Francis Drake, master mariner. He told them of the uncertainty of the future, the hardships that all would have to undergo; that success would depend largely upon each man striving, not for himself, but for the good of all; and that everyone on board from the captain to the ship's boy was in the hands of Almighty God. Finally, he gave them a motto for the voyage: 'Be ye all of one company'. What a motto for a voyage, for a Christian in the world, now.

All this mixed lot

But, you say, how can we be all of one company? We're utterly different from each other. Look at the person sitting next to you—(go on, do it now!). You're utterly different from him and probably quite glad to be! Some are parents: some are just starting school; others are fighting a national crisis called 'exams'; others are parsons. How can all this mixed lot be of one company? We can't, unless we have a common loyalty, unless we love the same thing we cannot be true to the motto of the Golden Hind.

The Christian's badge

Now comes the Christian's badge.

Do you remember the very first time you ever went to church? I doubt it, for you were probably a small baby in your mother's arms; and the only part you took in the service was to scream. But your godmother put you into the arms of the priest, and he, pouring water over your forehead in the great Name of the Trinity, Father, Son and Holy Spirit, and making the sign of the Cross on it, said some of the most wonderful words in the English language . . . 'I sign you with the sign of the Cross (and then everyone joined in with him saying) to show that you must not be ashamed to confess the faith of Christ crucified, and manfully to fight under his banner against sin, the world and the devil, and to continue Christ's faithful soldier and servant unto your life's end'. And the Christian's badge, the Cross, was on your forehead for ever.

I was trying to explain this to a small boy aged four, whom I had to baptize. Thinking he might be frightened, I took him the day before into church, lifted him up on to the side of the font, and said: 'Now tomorrow, John, it will be just like this, except that daddy and mummy and all your friends will be here. But I shall lift you up, just as I have done now, dip my hand into this big bath and after pouring water over your forehead three times go like that on it . . . making the sign of the Cross.' That puzzled him.

'Will it hurt?' he asked. 'No', I replied, 'it won't hurt.'

'Will it be like sticky plaster?' he enquired.

'Oh no, it won't be like sticky plaster.'

Then, being only four, he asked eagerly: 'Can I have a bandage on it afterwards?' But his mother, seeing me floundering, said: 'John, you won't be able to see it, or feel it, but it will always be there.' The badge on your forehead, you can't feel it or see it, but it will always be there.

Never alone

And do you know what it is? It is the badge of all those people throughout the whole world who are prepared to stand up as you so often do, and say: 'I believe in God Almighty . . . with God by my side I can dare and dare to the utmost'. Never think you are alone when you say this, or only with the people in the church beside you. They are saying it all over the world, in Her Majesty's ships at sea; they are saying it in our southernmost cathedral in the Falkland Islands; they are saying it in Wedaun in the New Guinea hills; in Zululand in Africa. In thousands of places all over the world, joining with angels and archangels, a great band of people, all of one company, all with the Christian's badge on their foreheads, are proclaiming their faith in the God they serve.

The question

Now comes the Question. There's only one. It's this . . . can *you* be loyal to the badge you bear? And only two people will know the answer, God and you.

Will you remember:

> The Golden Hind.
> The Christian's Badge.
> The Question.

SCHOOL LEAVERS

Five tests of vocation

Years ago a Dean of Winchester said that he thought there were five tests as to whether a man or woman had found their vocation in life. He had applied these tests over a period of a week to the people he had met, and these people had passed his tests: a preparatory schoolmaster, a maternity nurse, a working mother, with five sons, and a Nun of an enclosed Order. These were his tests . . . sparkling eyes—an eager spirit—sense of humour—an efficiency in the organisation of life—and a thrill of enthusiasm.

(1) Will you consider them? *Sparkling eyes* . . . No it's not just a matter of taking a pair of sparkling eyes. It will depend what you are looking at. It is not likely that your eyes will

sparkle as you behold what you personally conceive to be the faults in this or that government, the welfare state, the National Health Service or the management and direction of some concern—be it commercial, political, administrative or social—in which you don't have as great a hand as your personal assessment of your own abilities would seem to demand. It is certain that tepid and polite humanism will not fill your eyes with anything but baffled doubt. While there will be no hint of sparkle in the eyes of a business man who is so absorbed in the minor irritating characteristics of other members of his business undertaking that he has no time to discipline his own body and soul. The eyes must sparkle with the reflection of a great light. 'I will lift up mine eyes unto the hills from whence cometh my help; my help cometh even from the Lord.'

'Dost thou see yonder wicket gate?' says Evangelist to Christian in *Pilgrim's Progress*.

'No.'

'Dost thou see yonder shining light?'

'I *think* I do'; for remember Christian is an English business man and doesn't want to commit himself too deeply, so he cautiously says: 'I think I do.'

'"Keep yonder shining light in thine eye, and approach directly thereto; so shalt thou see the gate, at which when thou knockest it shall be told thee what thou must do." And I saw in my dream that the man began to run.' First then, sparkling eyes.

(2) *An eager spirit.* Which means energetic thinking, decisive action. This is the type of character that Jesus admires . . . the widow who would have justice; the vigorous man who found treasure and made use of it; the friend at night who hammered and hammered and hammered till he got his loaves; the man who would hack off his hand to enter into life.

Over against this eager spirit is the life of drift, waiting with Macawber-like optimism for something to turn up. There they were, said Jesus, in the days of Noah, eating, drinking, dreaming, marrying, and the Flood came and destroyed them. There is the man who everlastingly says and does not do. There is the business man who is always putting his religion in the pending basket. When he is a boy he is going to attend to it when he's passed his O Levels; then his A Levels; then when he has got into his firm or university; then when he has finished courting; then when the children are out in the world. And then one day in middle life he wakes up and finds that having given no answer to Christ he has in fact answered 'No'. There is the man so set in his ways who believes that what was good enough when he was young is good enough now. All these want to continue in a life of drift. 'No', says Christ. 'I demand energy of mind, I demand an eager spirit . . . with me or against me.'

(3) *A sense of humour*. Whenever I am asked for a reference I always look to see whether the writer wishes to know whether the candidate has a sense of humour. And if there is no such question I always make it my business to state whether or not the candidate is equipped with this precious gift. Anyone who dares to say that Christ had no sense of humour merely shows himself an unimaginative biblical scholar. For consider . . . ninety-nine just persons . . . can't you see his face as he said it? Can't you see the picture—all ninety-nine of them sitting in a row, just persons, smug and splendid, fiddling with their phylacteries, thumbing the Church newspapers, counting candles, while the great redemptive work of Christ goes on and the hound of heaven pursues the soul of man down the ages, going after the harlot and the sinner with overwhelming love.

It is surely essential for every business man, indeed every man who claims to be an active Christian, to cultivate his sense of humour continually and be able to rock with laughter at himself, especially when middle-age—what the psalmist calls the sickness that destroys in the noon-day—tends to harden the arteries of the conscience and we take ourselves too seriously.

(4) *Efficiency in the organisation of life*. Not, please note, life spent in the organisation of efficiency. Unlike the nurse or the school teacher your life is not likely to be ordered by a routine of bells, schedules and duties, holidays and terms. More likely it is to be in danger of being obsessed with the world, the flesh and the telephone. But if you are to be efficient in the organisa-tion of life, real life, life as Christ offers it, then you must have

vision, and to have vision you must have prayer. Would you agree with me that there is no time perhaps in this century when we have so badly needed men of vision who can lead us at every level of our common life? And I repeat, I believe to have vision you must have prayer. You will not need me to say that unless you have a set time to pray, in spite of all your duties, then you will have no time to pray.

(5) *A thrill of enthusiasm* for the job you have chosen, no, the job that has chosen you. Listen to a nurse, a mid-wife at one of our big London Hospitals: 'I have just done my first delivery by myself. Of course, Sister was standing by in case anything went wrong. It is the most wonderful thrill to feel that all one's training leads up to this ... so completely satisfying.' Watch the real teacher at his work; see the face of the seaman at his wheel; the young naval Officer on the bridge of his first command; catch the eye of the craftsman as he completes the really perfect bit of work, or the eye of the organist as he faces the console of a splendid instrument ... it is plain they are not of man's making; or read Pascal's diary on the day of what he called his conversion. At the top of the page the words 'Fire! Fire! Fire!' In the middle of the page 'Joy! Joy! Joy!' At the bottom of the page ... the cause of it all ... 'JESUS CHRIST'.

There then are the five tests. Perhaps you will try them on yourself ... sparkling eyes ... an eager spirit ... a sense of humour ... efficient organisation of life ... a thrill of enthusiasm. So, I ask you, have you found your vocation?

A MARRIAGE

I want you both to remember one word. It is the meaning of the Christian marriage service in which we have all just taken part. The word is *loyalty*.

Three kinds of loyalty

First—Loyalty to the best in each of you
John, it was the best in you that first attracted Mary. Mary,

it was the best in you that John fell in love with. And on your wedding day you determine that with God's help, in five, ten, twenty years' time you will continue to do all those little things for each other that you loved to do when you were courting. That is loyalty to the best in each of you.

The second loyalty is to each other
It sounds so obvious, doesn't it? But every married couple here knows just how much it means to both of them when they are separated, to be certain that no matter what happens both will be absolutely loyal.

Notice that in Christian marriage, loyalty to each other, loyalty of husband and wife to each other, must come first, absolutely first. So, John, don't allow anyone on this side of the church, however much they love you . . .

Mary, don't allow anyone on your side of the church, however much they love you, to interfere with your married life. And when you have children—as please God you will—and all your relations gather round and give you advice on how to bring them up, listen to it most politely but don't on any account take it! For it is to you two that God will give children, and it is to you two that they must look for their upbringing.

And the third loyalty?
It concerns the chief guest at your wedding—Almighty God. It is loyalty to him that keeps the other loyalties bright. To his house you have come on your wedding day to seek his blessing. For his strength you have prayed that you may keep those tremendous vows. Again and again you must come back to him for strength, for guidance, for vision, as your married life unfolds. Your children must learn his name—the name of Jesus—from you. No school, no Sunday School, no radio or television can take the place of parents. If mother and father pray, the children will pray. The family that prays together stays together.

There then are the three loyalties—loyalty to the best in each of you . . . loyalty to each other . . . and loyalty to God. May he on your wedding day most richly bless you both.

A MARRIAGE REUNION

Jesus was there

'There was a wedding at Cana in Galilee' (John 2.1)

Jesus and his disciples were invited to the marriage. Why? Because the bride and bridegroom wanted him there. They knew Jesus. They were friends of his. They were completely at home with him and couldn't have their wedding without him. So were some of their relations and friends. But not all. Some were really rather embarrassed when he walked in to the reception. Others wanted to talk to him so that they could tell their friends they had met a celebrity.

Some of the women noted his clothes, how his garment was seamless, woven from the top throughout.

Others were so worried about the reception that they didn't give Jesus more than a passing glance.

The bride's mother was thrilled to see Jesus—glad that her daughter and her new son-in-law had made friends with him. Now he'd come to their wedding, and then—Oh dear—she'd run out of drinks, just when she wanted everything to go right.

Soon the whisper went round among the women . . . 'run out of drinks'. One of them was Mary, the mother of Jesus of Nazareth. She understood the situation at once. She mentioned it to her son. He put it right. The bride's mother never forgot. Years after she used to tell her friends all about it. All was well —and the bride and her bridegroom weren't worried. It was their wedding day—and Jesus was there.

Later on

After their marriage, they used to listen to Jesus talking. They invited him to their home. It was only a little place, of course, but he seemed to fit in perfectly. He taught them how to pray. They used to do it together—just simply.

Later on, they were up in Jerusalem when he was condemned to death. They tried to stick up for him but people laughed at them. The chaps at work thought all that this fellow said was all right, but it just wouldn't work, it wasn't practical.

They saw him die. The bride, with a woman's eye, remembered with a sudden pang that that same seamless robe for which the soldiers were gambling was the one he'd worn at her wedding.

They never forgot that day. It was a Friday.

Later on still, when the children came, they told them all about Jesus. They taught them to pray, quite simply, and they all used to pray together, father, mother, John and Mary. They called the girl Mary after Jesus's mother, and the boy John—it meant a 'gift from God'.

Somehow it seemed as though Jesus was a member of the family—you couldn't see him, but he was always there.

But all this was in the future. At the moment there was a wedding in Cana of Galilee and Jesus was there.

Your wedding

It was just the same at your wedding, wasn't it? Jesus was there. You were friends of his, so were some of your relations and friends. But not everyone in the church felt at home. Some were rather embarrassed. Some thought a 'church wedding was so nice'. Some were only really interested in the bride's dress and what the bridesmaids looked like.

There were some pretty anxious moments planning the reception and getting the numbers right. But it was all right on the day. The drinks didn't run out. The bride's mother really loved the service. She was glad that her daughter and new son-in-law had naturally chosen to be married in their parish church. Everyone knew them there—they were quite at home. It was all very moving—Jesus was there.

Later on

And after your marriage . . . what about then? Is Jesus invited to share your home? At work do you stick up for him? It is the same Christ who is crucified. Do you mark that day? It is Good Friday.

Later on, since the children came, have you been bringing them up in the fear and nurture of the Lord . . . to know and love Jesus Christ? Do you go with them and others on a Sunday to worship as a family? Is it true to say that he really is a member of your family and that you are his friends?

Well, only three people know the true answer to these questions. You two, and God.

Now

But whether you answer with shame or gladness, such is his love that now, for you, Jesus is here.

> He is here to forgive your failures . . .
> when you've hurt each other,
> when you've sulked and refused to make it up,
> when you've given way to jealousy,
> when you've been unfaithful in thought or deed,
> when you've shirked your duties . . .

To forgive all this, Jesus is here. He's here to bless you again; to hallow all your best selves; to tell you to go on; to face and overcome daily difficulties together; to come into your home, to abide with you, just because he thinks the world of you.

As at your wedding, so now, Jesus is here.

FOR PARENTS

Bringing up parents

INTRODUCTION

Palaces have produced wicked villains and cottages have produced saints. Everyone knows this. People need good health and good houses but, like patriotism, they are not enough. We are to bring up our children, that is future parents, 'in the fear and nurture of the Lord'. 'Nurture', 'nourishment', they are both good words, though we are apt to forget the first in our concentration on diet and food values. But we are to train our children for heaven, and if we neglect their heavenly food, we may one day see them with stunted souls in well-nourished bodies.

Five duties

(1) I suggest that one of your first duties as parents is to do all
you can to see that your children do not make God too small.
Do you agree that we have been at times so precious in our
picture books for small children, in our suggested prayer books
and prayers, that children are encouraged to think that they can
know all there is to know about God? When they outgrow
their childish ideas they tend to out-grow God. That is why I
believe it is important to have definite statements such as are
splendidly set out in the Revised Catechism. These are easily
memorised and provide an effective safeguard against sloppy
thinking when, very rightly, our ideas develop and we need to
know that what we have been taught are not childish illusions
but the facts of the Faith.

(2) Secondly, if the fear of the Lord is the beginning of wisdom, and this fear is no abject terror of an unknown power but
the wholesome respect and awe for a trusted authority, I suggest
that this is best learnt by a small child through respect for his
father who is the final authority a child knows.

If we are going to teach our children, as we promise at their
baptism, the Lord's Prayer, 'Our Father', it seems to me that
we put a very heavy responsibility on fathers. Yes, I know all
the reasons why most of the religious upbringing, teaching in
prayer, etc., may at first have to be left to mother, simply
because father may not be at home in time, or go off too early.
We men are expert in talking about the Brotherhood of Man,
the Brotherhood of the Trade Unions, or Rotary or the Ancient
Order of Buffaloes; but what sort of God, what sort of father-
hood is conveyed to your child's mind by *your* behaviour?

One thing is certain. The father who will do anything to
avoid a row, the father who will seek popularity at all costs,
does less than nothing to give the child or young person an
adequate idea of the God Christians worship. God protects us
often against inexperience and ignorance. God says no—ask
yourself how often that has happened in your own life; earthly
fathers must copy their heavenly father in this. Listen to a
delightful, natural, and wholly adorable girl on the eve of her

wedding. 'We had a good home, no poverty or cruelty or quarrels, very much not. A good middle-class home, full of kindness and yet we got everything wrong. I never remember being made to do anything. We ought to have been told, not asked. How can children choose for themselves when they don't know anything? Well, I suppose we chose badly! I shall tell my children what's right and what's wrong so when they grow up they will have something to hold on to.'

'Something to hold on to.' Isn't that what the Christian faith should be?

(3) Thirdly, while learning to fear God through earthly respect for an earthly father, please note that in a Christian home, Christian parents are just as often wrong as children. As Christianity, the Christian life, is a way of walking, not of talking, we are all likely to err, we are all learning the way to God together. This, I believe, is one of the best features of our generation of parents, that we are prepared to admit to our children we are wrong. And Christian parents are prepared to admit to God they are wrong.

'Did you mind my making my confession?' said a prep. school boy to his father. 'You know that church where I sometimes wait in the car for Mummy? Well that's where we both go to make our confession.' Pause, then: 'Oh, so we're all in it together.' What better description of Christians as a family on the road to the celestial city?

(4) Fourthly, there is the difficult art of 'letting go'. Every time I say those words 'God so loved . . . he gave', I always seem to hear at least one lesson for parents. Just as God is not possessive in the narrow sense: just as God gave us free will: just as he gave us his Son wholly and completely though still close to him in inexpressible love and supremely intimate connection, so Christian parents have to let their children go. Are mothers worse at this? If so, study our Lord's mother. She seemed always to be there, but unobtrusively so. Even at the cross, as Augustine says: 'We read she stood, we do not read she wept'. As if to express an unutterable dignity in appalling suffering. Just because we love we tend to protect and cling.

God gives completely. He gives us everything he can to develop our personalities to the utmost, but he never does anything for us we should do ourselves. Yet all the while God *abides*. He is.

(5) And here is my fifth point. Christian parents must love and love and love. They must pray and pray and pray. Their children must know that just as their parents are in love with each other—and that with each other they come first (forsaking *all* other, remember), so no matter what the children do, no matter how *avant garde* or difficult (sometimes different names for the same behaviour) they may be, their parents will always love them, pray for them and believe in them, even when they don't deserve it in the slightest. 'Fear him ye saints and you will then have nothing else to fear' must be translated into family life in this way . . . that, come what may, your earthly father and mother will reflect the God who abides, who cares, who believes in what you can be at your best.

SUMMARY

But if I were asked to attempt to sum up the most important legacy which parents could give to their children I should try and say something like this:

Teach them that the Christian religion means saying 'yes' to life. That it is not just a matter of hard and fast rules like the old Law but that Christ has given us touchstones in his parables, his teaching, his life. Show them by your example that being a Christian is always an exciting experience, demanding all that the intellect, emotion and will can give in a concerted effort to seek God's will and to do it. Show them that worship, yes of course including Sunday worship, is a corporate activity, a creative and joyful activity. Show them that there will be hard bits, that religion without hard bits can never be the Christian religion, but that 'through all the changing scenes of life' God is, God loves, God cares, and that despite all the miserable mistakes and failures of your own life you have found this to be true. On a tablet in a Washington church a large modern family placed these few words as an epitaph to their father: 'In him we saw the reflection of our Heavenly Father'. Could parenthood want or win higher praise?

FOR MEN

The great question

'And you' he asked, *'who do you say I am?'* (Matthew 16.15)

'Come and play with me, Daddy', said a small boy to his father who was busy working in his study. 'I can't just now, I'm busy.' But the boy persisted. 'Here', said the father, 'here's a puzzle. I think you will enjoy it. When you've managed to do it you will find there's a wonderful map of the world.' The boy took the puzzle, slammed the door and was gone. All too soon there was the sound of flying feet. The door opened. 'Look, Dad, I've done it.' 'You have been quick', said the father. 'How did you manage to do it so soon?' 'Well you see, Dad, on the other side of the map of the world was a map of a man; and when I got the man right the world came right, too.'

So let's be quite clear. It's you and me we are concerned with. It's not the Church, it's not the bishops, it's not the Government, it's not any mysterious 'they'. Some say he's Elijah, a prophet; some say he's John the Baptist; some say he's a good man; some say his ethics are good. Yes, but you, it's you he asks, you Peter and John, Smith and Jones and Robinson—men of the Church of England, 'Who do you say that I am?'

And you must answer in three ways.

1. *Your own holiness*

By your own holiness. Yes, I said 'holiness'. By your own worship, your own 'wholeness', that is, your own total response to all that God has done and is doing for you and mankind through Jesus Christ.

'Dad, what does your communion mean to you?'

'Dad, tell us how you say your prayers?'

'Dad, why do you read the Bible every day?'

'Dad, why don't you ever read the Bible?'

'Dad, why do we only say Grace when the Vicar calls and Mum kicks you under the table to remind you to ask him to do so?'

'Dad, do you think this idea of "till death us do part" is a good idea in marriage?'

'Dad, why is it when you and mum have a row she always apologises and you don't?'

Are these questions from your son, your nephew, your godson, the sort of questions you can answer without shame or embarrassment? If not, why not? Because no amount of synods, conferences, petitions, motions, resolutions, lobbying, projects, programmes, societies will avail one whit if you personally are not seen to be and to have been 'with Jesus'. If your relationship to Christ makes no difference, a difference hard to define perhaps, but clearly felt and recognised by your family, your friends and your business associates, then the first way in which you have answered Christ's question, 'and you, whom do you say I am?' will be a hollow sham of a mere respectability that is founded on the sand of conventional religiosity, not on the rock which is Christ.

Your first answer must be your own holiness.

2. Understand your faith

You must answer with an understanding of your faith.

Come to Southwark Cathedral just after the war. Cuthbert Bardsley was, as Provost of that cathedral, building up a lunch-hour ministry with business men—a heritage into which I and other Provosts later on gratefully entered. He had finished one series of lunch-hour addresses and the Committee was discussing the next. They had had Christianity and Communism, Christianity and Work, Christianity and Politics, Christianity and this, Christianity and that. Then someone asked 'Couldn't we have a series on Christianity?' He was surely right; I believe he would be more right now. Never before has the need for instructed lay Christians seemed so great.

Do *you* study? Do you feed your mind with some straight-forward books on Christian topics?

Can you personally offer to your friends Christian insights founded on Christ's teaching on leisure, marriage, personal relationships, the difference between pornography and whatsoever things are lovely? Can you interpolate the consideration of Christian values and questions of culture, art, literature, international friendship into the solely material deliberations about the Common Market? Have you as a Christian anything to say about abortion, euthanasia, housing, industrial relations?

You have? Good. But it must be Christ's teaching, not your prejudices. And remember we worship a God who makes all things new and it is his Holy Spirit that hammers at closed minds, entrenched prejudices and partisan policies.

You answer Christ's question by your own holiness, and by your own knowledge of the Christian faith. And, thirdly, by your participation in everyday life at a domestic, local and national level to expound, disseminate and practise Christian standards.

3. *Christian involvement*

Make no mistake. The charges against our generation which our sons make are formidable. We resent their revolt. You may dislike their methods. But you have no right to overlook the fact that the average age of the fathers of university students is now between 45 and 55, and that the new older generation was born between 1918 and 1930.

How do our younger generation sum up the charges against us? Ugliness? Guilty. Commercialism? Guilty. Dark and palsied materialism? Guilty. Racial prejudice? Guilty. Worldly prudence? Guilty. Neglect of world and British poverty? Guilty. Technological arrogance? Guilty. Organisational gigantism? Guilty. De-humanisation? Guilty. Family isolation? Guilty. Boredom? Guilty. Universal dullness reigns over all? Well, what do you think, guilty or not guilty?

But we are not here to bemoan what is wrong. We are here to plan how in God's strength we can make our contribution to putting things right.

I believe we can each one of us make a contribution if we are prepared to answer clearly Christ's question 'who do you say that I am?' God wants the best Christians in every job. He wants the doctor who remembers that his patients have souls as well as bodies; the Christian Member of Parliament, local councillor, government official who tries to promote good laws. He wants Christian businessmen who in all their dealings remember that they are dealing with individuals and not just digits. He wants businessmen whose word is their bond. He wants Christian journalists, script-writers and camera men. He wants Christian secretaries and telephonists who realise they are helping people to meet people. He wants Christian men and women who dare to share Christ's title of 'teacher'; Christian factory, engineering, farm workers; Christians who are not ashamed to confess the faith of Christ crucified in the armed forces of the Crown; Christian clippies and bus-drivers; Christian parents who do a wonderful piece of church-work training their children for heaven; Christian grandparents who exhibit that most difficult of arts, growing old gracefully. In short he wants people who are alive to their vocation as Christians, doing the job God wants them to do with all their might.

Your own holiness.
Your understanding of the Christian Faith.
Your witness to Christian standards.

These must be your clear answers when Christ asks you:
'And you—who do you say I am?'

FOR WOMEN

Spring-cleaning

'*Cast clouts and rotten rags*' (Jeremiah 38.6-12)

INTRODUCTION

Spring-cleaning, a time of year when, as someone has said, the wife steers the domestic ship through a storm of dust while the husband, with scarcely a life-belt left to hand, prays for calmer weather!

Yet no one who reads history can suppose that this activity of spring-cleaning is a new thing. Look for a moment at the story of our text. Jerusalem is surrounded by a besieging army of Babylonians. Jeremiah is arrested on a false charge of deserting to the enemy and is kept in custody; and then, when the influential courtiers have over-persuaded King Zedekiah who wished to befriend the prophet, he is let down by cords into a dungeon where there is no water but mire. 'He sank in the mire.' Then Ebed-melech pleaded for the old prophet and the King, yielding always to the last comer, ordered his release to take place. On his way to the dungeon Ebed-melech goes to collect some cast clouts and rotten rags from a cellar under the king's treasury. How had these rags got there? Surely it needs very little imagination to visualise the annual spring-cleaning of the palace. The royal wardrobe and those of the courtiers are carefully inspected and anything which is even slightly worn is cast off and taken away to be used for the palace furnaces. But these cast clouts and rotten rags have not reached the furnace. How is that? Because as today, so then, some shrewd and careful woman has visualised occasions when cast clouts might 'come in useful' and so has neatly folded the rags into piles, easy of access to any who should chance to enter the cellar.

Just such an eventuality as she had foreseen has now occurred, and Ebed-melech on his way to release Jeremiah wishes to temper mere justice with charity, to soften the chafing cords. He goes into the cellar under the treasury to see if he can find anything suitable. Cast clouts and rotten rags are the very things for his purpose; and binding these round the cords, and with the aid of his band of men, he draws up the old prophet from the miry dungeon, and frees him for further service and leadership.

And now

All this happened 700 years before Christ. Now let us come down the centuries to our own times. There has been a great deal of national and international spring-cleaning recently, hasn't there? Many clouts have been cast, of creeds and morals, of standards and ideals. But let us not look abroad, let us turn to our own land, and go down into the cellars and storehouses. In the dim light we can discern a considerable collection of waste material. It is divided into neat piles. One corner is labelled 'National Costumes'. Let us see what sort of clouts the nation has cast.

(1) Here is a piece of gold brocade, simple, solid, and lasting. It is labelled 'Christian Morality'. Why has it been discarded? We ask the kindly soul who has arranged and tended the storehouse. 'Ah', she says, 'you may well ask that. They seem to use a new kind of material now, more gaudy and flashy, but cheap and short-wearing. "The New Morality" they call it. It is made by a firm called "The Modern Outlook Company", and their slogan is "Why shouldn't I?" And look at that piece of stuff so ragged and torn. It's a composite material made up of two kinds of stuff, "The Sanctity of Marriage" and "Home Life". As soon as one wears out the other is rotted and useless.'

(2) Now we turn to another corner of the cellar and there are bundles labelled 'Individual Costumes'. Here is a piece of material once pure white; the name of it is 'Confirmation Vow'. Now it is faded and frayed, cast off and forgotten. And there in that other corner is a huge stack of quiet-coloured material, seemingly in good condition, but apparently unwanted and discarded. 'Yes', says the woman, 'we get so much of that cast off now. It is not considered exciting enough; it's really used to strengthen the other materials. You can't make anything without it. It's called "Private Prayer".'

(3) We turn to look at the faithful soul who tends with such loving care the cast clouts and rotten rags. She is old, yet her eye is not dim; lines of hardship and experience show on her face, but she is full of vigour; her hands are active, and her expression is compassionate.

We ask her who she is. 'They call me "Mother Church". Often people come to me and for one reason or another want to cast off their coat of childlike faith; they are lonely, they feel themselves unloved, they seem so unimportant in the world.

I try to encourage them, and often, very often, I succeed. But even if they cast their cloak away, I know the real value of these things—Christian Morality, the Confirmation Vow, the Home Life—cast clouts though they may be.'

They are stored in a cellar—yes—but the cellar of the king's treasury. No ordinary king this, no vacillating Zedekiah with the cunning of a Herod and the weakness of a Pilate. But a king 'with whom is no variableness nor shadow of turning', a king upon whose eternal changelessness we can surely rest.

Those cast clouts were waiting for the king's messenger to come on his mission of love to rescue man from the mire of sin.

He came. And then, unlike the hero of this Old Testament story, unlike any other hero, he suffered more deeply than suffering humanity itself. He rose on Easter morning. Then with his little band of followers he touches for his own our cast clouts and rotten rags. He binds them round with cords of love and draws humanity from the miry dungeon of despair into the kingdom of his marvellous light. And humanity means—you and me.

> Out of that place of dust
>   Life yet sufficed.
> O hearts of men, shall we not trust
>   The Tree of Christ?
>
> Dying to find new birth,
>   Wide-armed He waits;
> And all the storms of earth
>   Shake not those gates!

AT A DEDICATION FESTIVAL

The Church Christ would like to see

'Why don't you preach a sermon on "The Church I would like to see"?' someone asked me the other day. I promised I would. And our Dedication Festival seemed the right time to do it.

But it doesn't really matter about what *I* would like to see.

What matters is what sort of Church Christ would like to see.

Let's be quite clear about one thing right at the start. When I say 'Church' I mean that body of people that has at least three members—quite apart from all the rest—Christ and you and me.

I believe the Church that Christ would like to see would be:

Lively. One. Virile. Expectant.

(1) *Lively*—not just living. I've met not a few people who are 'living' but you could hardly call them 'lively'. I turn to the Oxford Dictionary and find: 'Lively . . . full of life, realistic, vigorous, energetic, vivid, interesting, exciting, dangerous, difficult.' 'I came', said Christ, 'that they might have life and have it in full measure.'

Is our worship exciting? If not, why not? Is it joyful? Are we alive to change, changing situations, changing patterns of society, the temptation of too much pastoral thinking in urban surroundings? Are we alive to new patterns of thought, new temptations, new idols masquerading as gods instead of *the* God we trust? Is our Christian religion infectious?

(2) *One*. I don't want the unity of all Christian people because some people think it is a good idea or a financial saving, or organisationally tidy. I want unity because it is the will of God, because it was Christ's prayer that we all might be one. What am I doing about it? How much do I know about the beliefs, forms of worship and problems of faith of my friends and acquaintances of other denominations? Are there things which we Anglicans are doing in this parish that could be much better done with Christians of other Churches?

(3) *Virile*. The Oxford Dictionary again . . . 'having pro-creative power; having masculine vigour or strength.'

That means not being apologetic about your Christianity. Your Creed doesn't begin . . . 'I venture to think that the possibility is that behind the universe there is a something which we might under certain circumstances not be too inaccurate in referring to as a possible first cause . . .' No. Your Creed begins . . . 'I believe in God . . .'

You must be able to give a reason for the faith that is in you. Why do you make your communion? What is your rule of life, of prayer, of Bible-reading, alms-giving, self-examination?

Can your Christianity stand up to hard knocks and possibly ridicule at work? Is it virile?

(4) *Expectant.* Have you noticed that we only seem to use this word nowadays of expectant mothers? I believe that Christ wants his Church to have just that expectancy that the mother has who is eagerly looking forward to this miracle of birth, this miracle for which she and her husband prayed at their wedding. So the Christian Church, and the part of it in this parish, must be expectant. Expect miracles to happen. Expect lives to be changed by the power of Christ. Expect Christ to show us through thought and prayer what the next step should be for ourselves and our parish, our country and our Church.

Lively.

One.

Virile.

Expectant.

You've noticed. The first letters spell the one great invincible and Christlike word—LOVE.

The Church Christ would like to see would be just that.

AT A CIVIC OCCASION

'The multitude was divided' (Acts 23.6-8)

The multitude was divided. So were the council. Some believed in the resurrection. Some didn't. That was in AD 64. In AD 197- it is exactly the same. The multitude are divided. In a recent survey out of one hundred people who admitted that they had gone to church on Easter Day, one in four did not believe in immortality. Six out of ten in England say they have never read the Bible; and only one in seven admits to going to church or chapel.

So the multitude have been divided down history. As then, so now. Christ told us bluntly that it would be so. Opinions about him would differ. They always have. This is the age of labels. We talk about the Dark Ages and the Age of Faith. We talk of the Age of Reason and the Victorian Age. What shall we be called, we of the seventies? The schizophrenic age?

Never before have people known so much about themselves. Their reflexes, inhibitions, reactions, complexes, subconscious. Never before have they been so frightened of what they have discovered.

Never before has man achieved so much in the mastery of his surrounding universe. Never before has he been so appalled at what he has achieved and the possible consequences of his discoveries.

Perhaps some future historian will prefer to call this the age of fear. Fear of war, of insecurity, fear of disease, fear of loneliness, fear of the dark, fear of old age.

The answer to an age of fear is an age of faith that is virile, sane and firm. Have we got that? Well, the multitude is divided. So, you notice, was the council. As then, so now. Some have got this faith. Only a few *claim* to be non-believers. The others claim to have some allegiance to God. Some come to no conclusions and delight in discussing the question, 'Whom do men say that I the Son of Man am?' in a dispassionate, academic sort of way.

But you have made a decision. I hope, Mr Mayor and Councillors, that your presence here proves that. I hope that you have come here as more than a civic duty. I hope that you are here because you believe that except the Lord build the city, the borough or the community, their labour is but lost that build it. I hope you believe, as I do, that the silent revolution through which we have lived called the Welfare State is something for which we should daily be profoundly thankful, but it is not, nor ever will be *of itself*, a vestibule to the kingdom of God.

I am not suggesting a pseudo-pious withdrawal of Christians from the affairs of clinic and council. Just the reverse. One of the most blasphemous sentences which I ever heard was spoken when the leader of a certain city council in England, opposing the use of prayer before the council meeting, said:

'You cannot mix religion and business'. It was to do precisely that that Christ came and lived and loved and died and rose.

Vital question

At once comes the crucial question which every councillor here must answer. Is the community a means to an end or an end in itself? This is the really ultimate question whether we are thinking of the state, of a collection of states, or of the borough, or the village.

Does the community exist for the sake of the individual or the individual for the community? The answer to both is 'No'. Both community and individual exist for God.

If you eliminate God, and, remember, councils and multitudes have tried to, you are confronted with clear alternatives— some form of totalitarianism or some form of self-interest or at best an uneasy tension between the two. This latter, I believe, is what we have in this country.

If, on the other hand, you see the whole thing in terms of God, then you see the community as a family of individuals.

The way ahead

Here, then, as I see it, is the real task of local government. It is not made easier by the tendency to exalt the State at the expense of both the smaller community and the individual. But if local government is to continue, not as a mere department of a large whole, but in a very real sense as a family affair, it has to preserve both the value of the individual and the concept of the family.

It can do so only on a specifically Christian basis, i.e. by recognising that it is the duty of the community to provide an atmosphere in which each individual can be the kind of person God intended him to be.

So in the detailed administration of a borough, the Council and its officers must always be looking beyond the neat pattern and orderly arrangement, beyond the house, the drain, the library, the school, the art exhibition, to the person, i.e. beyond the community to the individual. It is in the end the individual who counts in God's sight. Because he is created by God to be a son of God.

So I suggest to you all who are here today, that the test of all your work must be God's test for human society. Is this society and nation which we are fashioning going to make men, women and children living personalities, valuable in God's sight, better able to live as God meant them to, for he has called them children of God? Can this be done without a living, firm, virile, sane faith in God, in Jesus Christ and the power of his resurrection. In AD 64 the multitude were divided. So were the council. In AD 197- what do *you* say?

ST LUKE'STIDE, HOSPITALS ETC.

The man in the end bed

I haven't told you who I am. I'm the man in the end bed. J.C. are my initials. John Carter. I know this hospital well—have known it all my life. My mother used to tell me how one of its midwives on district brought me into the world—and the other seven in the family too; my own children were born here; the wife died here; I've been attending out-patients for years, and been in this ward a few times before this last one. Nearly always in this end bed.

What's it like? Well, it varies, you know. By the time you've been connected with the hospital as long as I, you've met all sorts.

But I think the one thing that sticks out a mile is the difference between those who treat you as a person and those who treat you as a case.

To some, porters, clerks, almoners—(they call them something else now)—I can see the expression on their faces: 'What! This old boy again!' Others of them greet me like a real old friend.

It's the same with the nurses. To some I'm just the man in the end bed—the man who always wants his pillows put just right at just the wrong moment, the man who is inclined to tell the day nurse that she doesn't get them as comfortable as the night nurse.

To others I seem to be someone—someone who really matters. It's not just that they call me 'Mr Carter'—always so polite—it's—well, it's their whole attitude.

It's the same with the doctors. There's the student. I've seen a few in my time, I can tell you. Some of them seem interested in me—all of me; and others who are mighty efficient, treat me as though I had no feelings; and they're always the ones who talk far too loudly about me and forget that by now I understand much more than they think.

Then there's the chiefs. Just the same there too. Most of them come into the ward like a battleship, with a destroyer-screen of registrars, housemen, students, Sisters and the rest. But in spite of all this you soon know that some really know and care for you.

That's how I used to see them. That's how I used to see the whole hospital.

I see them differently now. The Student who's unsure of himself; the Houseman who is desperately anxious to succeed and hasn't yet learned how to organise his work and manage his personal relationships; the Staff Nurse who always gave the impression that she had refused the matronship of five London Hospitals, (Chief Nursing Officer No. 10, 9, 8 and the rest!) but was really only finding it difficult to adjust herself to power; and the 'Pro' who's wondering whether she really has done right to do nursing, though she felt certain when she started that this was the one thing she was called to do. Yes, I see them quite differently now. Why? Let me tell you how it happened.

How it happened

One night I couldn't sleep, had quite a bit of pain. One of the night nurses came over to me and we got talking—you know how you do. She had been about the world a bit before she took up nursing. I think she knew I was not feeling too well. At any rate suddenly she said: 'Have you tried praying?' I didn't quite know what to say, for I've never had much to do with religion; it's not in my line somehow, and I always thought it best to pretend to be asleep when the chaplain's been about. But she

wasn't a bit embarrassed by my silence, and I heard her saying . . .
'I don't mean just praying for yourself, but for other people,
thinking about God for a bit instead of yourself?' I mumbled
something about not knowing how to go about it, and asked
wasn't it difficult.

She seemed to understand just how I felt. I shall never forget
what she told me. It was all so simple. I think I could repeat it
all almost word for word.

The method

'I don't find it easy to pray,' she said, 'and many of the books
I've read are too difficult for me. So this is how I pray for other
people. I use my right hand. It's usually doing something—
ironing, washing-up, making a bed, holding something—it
used to do a lot of strap-hanging before I started nursing! But
my thumb is nearest to me. So I pray for all those who are
nearest to me, all those I love wherever they are, my mother in
Paradise and my young brother in the army and my father who
is a country doctor.

'Then there's the next finger. That's the one that people
always point at me. The one they used to use at school when
they wanted me. So I pray for all those who teach me. The
Sister Tutor and the Staff Nurse of the Preliminary Training
School—how surprised they'd be—and Matron too, and those
engaged on medical research who are trying to help us cure
people like you.

'Then the third finger. That's the tallest. So I pray for the
V.I.P's, for those who run our country, the Queen and those in
authority . . . and remember, no cheating, you don't just pray
for the Government if it's the one you voted for. It's not a
question of "Please keep the Tories in" or "Please bring back
Labour". I wonder what it would mean for the Prime Minister
if every nurse, doctor, and patient in the land prayed for God's
blessing on him and his Cabinet every day?'

I was really interested by now. 'What about the fourth finger?'
I asked.

'Well, that's the weakest of the lot—you'd soon find that if you tried to play the piano. So I pray for the sick, all those in this ward whom I nurse, especially my old friend in the end bed.' That fairly shook me. I don't think I'd ever thought of anyone praying for me before.

'Then there's the little finger,' she went on, 'not very important. That's me—that's when I pray for myself, that I may do my job really well . . . though, of course, that comes after all the other prayers.

'Those I love,
Those who teach me,
The V.I.P's,
The sick,
Myself.

'It's a simple method, isn't it?' she said. 'My father taught it to me. He uses it when he's driving about the country on his rounds. It's about the only time he gets to say his prayers undisturbed. You've always got your right hand to help you. Other people have more time to pray. Perhaps you have?'

CONCLUSION

She didn't say any more. I got down to it right away. I managed to keep it up. She used to help me. It worked! I believe that's why I see people differently now. I seemed to spend most of my life before this thinking about myself. I believe God did help me. I know he did. I couldn't have died without him.

But I didn't expect to and myself in Paradise. Perhaps it was someone else's prayers.

Yes, I was just the man in the end bed. J.C. are my initials. They stand for John Carter. They might stand for Jesus Christ. For what they did in that hospital for me, with their prayers and their skill, they really did for him. I wonder if they know.

Do you?

FOR OLD PEOPLE

Growing old gracefully

'Don't you remember?' is, I suppose, one of the slogans of old age. The other day I happened to notice that while the word 'forget' occurs 73 times in the 39 books of the Old Testament, the word 'remember' can be found 61 times in the twenty-seven books of the New Testament.

So I want to talk to you today about old age.

But, first of all . . . what is old age? How are we to regard it? Is it a distasteful, regrettable finale to life? Or is it an age with a positive value; an age with an intrinsic beauty of its own?

The answer to these questions seems to me to depend on whether you regard this life as the end of everything; or whether you see it as just a time of preparation. But before I ask you whether you are growing old gracefully, I expect *you* may want to ask me, 'When do we become old?'

What do *you* think? Of course, one of our grandchildren will say, 'Mummy's very old, she must be at least thirty!' The medical world tells us that the age of maturity is twenty-five. Some say 'a man is as old as he feels' but that doesn't really get us very far. No, it's usually the body which tells us most about our age. Don't *you* find that? We tire more easily . . . those stairs . . . our memory isn't what it was . . . we can't describe a fact without going into a long rigmarole of details that led up to it . . . we begin to live in the past.

We must be quite clear about this next point. Just as we need preparation for life, so we need preparation for old age. We have to try and cultivate a new mental and spiritual outlook. The Chinese have a proverb which says:

> May your old age be like the evergreen pine,
> And its fragrance like the flower of the red camellia . . .

In other words, may you grow old gracefully . . . full of grace.

I hope you're saying to me . . . 'I'd like to grow old gracefully. I'd like to prepare for it properly.' Or, 'I'd like to start again. What do I do?'

Four ways to prepare

I'd say you've got to try and do four things. And they all begin with 'Don't you remember?'

(1) Don't you remember that in the letter to the Hebrews in

the New Testament we are told not to forget the assembling of ourselves together? Well, I expect you did that when you were hale and hearty. Perhaps you're one of those who still do. But if through infirmity or sickness you can't get to church as you used to, there's the wireless, the television. There's your Bible and Prayer Book. While others are at church, you can quietly be in your own room and join with them. Don't you remember our Lord saying: 'When thou prayest, go into thy room and shut thy door and pray to thy Father'?

(2) Don't you remember how Christ said: 'I have given you an example that ye shall do as I have done'? No brooding over past wrongs, slights or hurts. His love and forgiveness marked all his acts and words. How wonderful of him always to see some good in everybody and everything. So if you're in doubt, just ask yourself 'What would Jesus do?'

(3) Don't you remember how he said: 'Do this in remembrance of me'? As we grow older and more infirm we are inclined to forget this. Yet if you're confined to bed, your parish priest or minister will gladly come to you. As I look back on my ministry I value as much as anything those times when in a sick room, perhaps alone with one sick person, or with a friend, we carried out Christ's command . . . 'Do this in remembrance of me'.

(4) Don't you remember how he has told us: 'Lo, I am with you even unto the end'? So when the shadows of this world grow darker and longer, hold on to that. My sight is not as good as it used to be. Perhaps yours isn't either. But at the end of my life I want to say to him:

Hold thou thy Cross before my closing eyes;
Shine through the gloom, and point me to the skies:

and then because he's promised to be with me always, I think those last two lines need just a little change of wording. For me they read:

Heaven's morning breaks, and earth's vain shadows flee;
In life—in death, My Lord ABIDES with me.

And I believe I shall hear my Saviour whisper: 'Don't you remember that I told you this?'